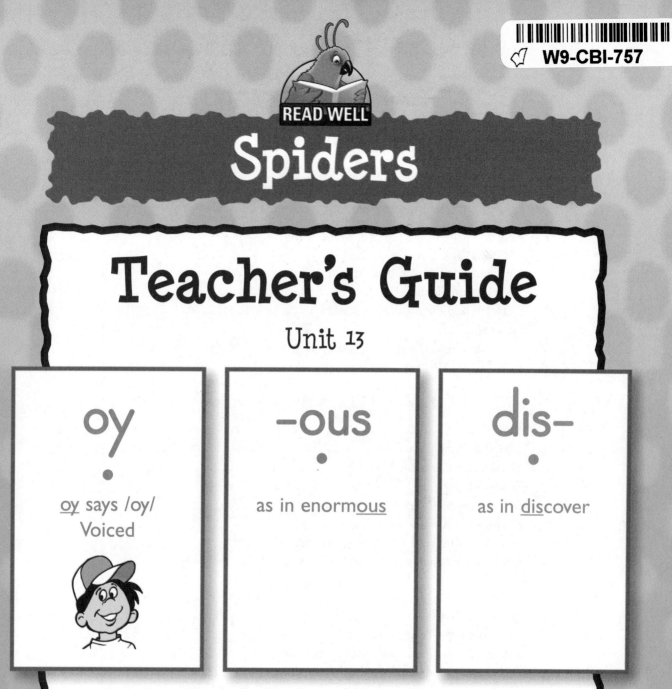

READ WELL

Spiders

Teacher's Guide

Unit 13

oy	-ous	dis-
oy says /oy/ Voiced	as in enorm<u>ous</u>	as in <u>dis</u>cover

Note: See New and Important Objectives on page 2 for a complete list of skills taught and reviewed.

Critical Foundations in Primary Reading

Marilyn Sprick, Ann Watanabe, Karen Akiyama-Paik, and Shelley V. Jones

Copyright 2009 Sopris West Educational Services. All rights reserved.

Sopris West®
EDUCATIONAL SERVICES

A Cambium Learning® Company

BOSTON, MA • LONGMONT, CO

ISBN 13-digit: 978-1-60218-536-4
ISBN 10-digit: 1-60218-536-0

7 8 9 10 11   B&B   16 15 14 13 12

166967/6-12

Table of Contents

Unit 13

Spiders

Letter Sounds and Combinations

Cumulative Review of *Read Well 1* Sounds and Combinations (Ss, Ee, ee, Mm, Aa, Dd, th, Nn, Tt, Ww, Ii, Th, Hh, Cc, Rr, ea, sh, Sh, Kk, -ck, oo, ar, wh, Wh, ĕ, -y as in fly, Ll, Oo, Bb, all, Gg, Ff, Uu, er, oo as in book, Yy, a schwa, Pp, ay, Vv, Qq, Jj, Xx, or, Zz, a_e, -y as in baby, i_e, ou, ow as in cow, ch, Ch, ai, igh, o_e, ir) and:

Unit 2	Unit 3		Unit 5	Unit 6
aw /aw/ **Paw** Voiced	**ew** /o͞o/ **Crew** Voiced	**ue** /o͞o/ **Blue** Voiced / **u_e** /o͞o/ **Flute** Bossy E Voiced	**ow** /ō͞ō/ **Snow** Voiced (Long)	**ge** /j/ **Page** Voiced

Unit 6	Unit 7		Unit 8		Unit 10
-dge /j/ **Badge** Voiced	**ci** /sss/ **Circle** Unvoiced	**ce** /sss/ **Center** Unvoiced	**kn** /nnn/ **Knee** Voiced	**ph** /fff/ **Phone** Unvoiced	**oa** /ō͞ō/ **Boat** Voiced (Long)

Unit 11		Unit 12		Unit 13
oi /oi/ **Point** Voiced	**ea** /ĕĕĕ/ **Bread** Voiced (Short)	**gi** /j/ **Giraffe** Voiced	**au** /au/ **Astronaut** Voiced	**oy** /oy/ **Boy** Voiced

Affixes (including morphographs—affixes taught with meaning) and Open Syllables

Cumulative Review of *Read Well 1* Affixes (-ed, -en, -es, -ing, -ly, -s, -y, -tion) and:

Unit 2	Unit 3		Unit 5		Unit 6
re- **Means again** as in **re**read	**un-** **Means not** as in **un**happy	**ex-** as in **ex**cited	**o** Open syllable /ō/ as in **o**pen and moment	**-ful** **Means full of** as in color**ful**	**bi-** **Means two** as in **bi**cycle

Unit 7	Unit 8	Unit 11	Unit 12	Unit 13	
de- as in **de**tective	**-able** as in comfort**able**	**i** Open syllable /ī/ as in s**i**lence and p**i**lot	**be-** as in **be**fore	**-ous** as in enorm**ous**	**dis-** as in **dis**cover

Unit 14		Unit 15		Unit 16	
-al as in anim**al**	**-ible** as in flex**ible**	**-or** **Means one who** as in act**or**	**-ment** as in apart**ment**	**-ic** as in scientif**ic**	**pre-** **Means before** as in **pre**view

Unit 17		Unit 18		Unit 19	
-ity as in activ**ity**	**-sion** as in permis**sion**	**-ness** as in fair**ness**	**-less** **Means without** as in help**less**	**in-** as in **in**sert	**im-** **Means not** as in **im**possible

Introduction
Spiders

Story Notes

The storybook *Spiders and Bats* is filled with interesting selections, photos, and bright illustrations that will intrigue your students. We paired expository selections about spiders and bats with American Indian legends in which the characteristics of the animal are used to teach a lesson.

Spider, Spider, on the Wall: This selection covers fascinating facts about the common but complex spider. Students will use knowledge gained through their reading to write their own spider reports.

Fun With Rhymes: Itsy Bitsy Spider and Jack and Jill are paired for another spill down the hill.

Centipede and Grandmother Spider: American Indians have used legends to pass their cultural heritage from one generation to the next. The legend "Centipede and Grandmother Spider" is told by a grandfather to his grandson.

Recommended Read Alouds

The *Read Well 2* suggested Read Alouds enhance small group instruction—providing opportunities to further build background knowledge and vocabulary.

CAUTION
Do not read the Read Aloud recommendations during small group instruction. Reserve this time for students to read.

The Diary of a Spider by Doreen Cronin
Fiction • Narrative
Students will enjoy this entertaining account of the adventures of a young spider.

Read Well Connections
Students can apply the facts they learn about spiders to explain entries in the spider's diary. At the end of this unit, your students will be able to explain why the spider's gym class meets on the basketball hoop!

NOTE FROM THE AUTHORS

RICH IN RELATED WRITING ACTIVITIES

Read Well 2 is not a writing program. Instead, writing is used as a tool to develop comprehension. By recording and writing about what they've read, your students will learn how to take command of a subject.

When your students finish their spider reports, be sure to celebrate their accomplishments. Reading their reports to the principal or volunteers, having their reports typed by volunteers, or making spider props can all highlight a job well done.

New and Important Objectives
A Research-Based Reading Program

Phonemic Awareness
Phonics
Fluency
Vocabulary
Comprehension

Phonological and Phonemic Awareness
Blending; Rhyming; Onset and Rime; Counting Syllables

Phonics
Cumulative Letter Sounds and Combinations
Review • Ss, Ee, ee, Mm, Aa, Dd, th, Nn, Tt, Ww, Ii, Th, Hh, Cc, Rr, ea, sh, Sh, Kk, -ck, oo, ar, wh, Wh, ĕ, -y (as in fly), Ll, Oo, Bb, all, Gg, Ff, Uu, er, oo (as in book), Yy, a (schwa), Pp, ay, Vv, Qq, Jj, Xx, or, Zz, a_e, -y (as in baby), i_e, ou, ow (as in cow), ch, Ch, ai, igh, o_e, ir, aw, ew, ue, u_e, ow (as in snow), ge, -dge, ci, ce, kn, ph, oa, oi, ea (as in bread), gi, au

Cumulative Affixes, Morphographs, and Open Syllables
Review • -ed, -en, -er, -es, -est, -ing, -ly, -s, -y, -tion, re-, un-, ex-, o (as in open), -ful, bi-, de-, -able, i (as in silence), be-

☆New Letter Sounds, Combinations, Affixes, and Morphographs
oy (as in boy) • annoy, employ, enjoy, Roy's, soy, toy
-ous (as in enormous) • poisonous, mountainous
dis- (as in discover) • display

☆New Proper Nouns
Centipede, Creator, Grandmother Spider Itsy Bitsy, Wolf

☆New Pattern Words
breeze, burn, burning, cave, caves, crab, creep, crown, dew, dried, etch, fang, fangs, fetch, fifth, flies, hawk, itch, jerk, mouse, orb, pads, pail, pails, pass, peak, peal, peep, plates, scales, shrimp, sketch, snores, spout, steel, trap, trapped, traps, twig, twigs, weave, weaving, wheel, woke, wound, yum

---

* **Known Pattern Words With Affixes, Known Tricky Words With Affixes,** and **Known Multisyllabic Words With Affixes**
have base words students have previously read. The words are new in this unit because they have not been previously read with the affix.

☆ = New in this unit

Phonics (continued)

*__Known Pattern Words With Affixes__ • bee's, bites, catching, closely, darted, deeply, digging, drops, eaten, forms, hairs, hears, hides, holes, hooked, lakes, lines, messed, noisy, pairs, passes, rehooked, rushes, saves, senses, shapes, sheds, sizes, smartest, smelling, spokes, sticky, stronger, tasting, thickness, threads, toads, tricky, types, unlike, waits, webs, winged

☆__New Compound and Hyphenated Words__

backbone, cobweb, cobwebs, cold-blooded, dewdrops, downpour, dragline, draglines, eight-legged, grasshopper, homework, know-it-all, rattlesnake, spiderweb, themselves, therefore, tonight, waterspout, waterspouts

☆__Other New Multisyllabic Words__

ability, amphibian, amphibians, angry, attics, awake, beetle, belly, bitsy, buzzard, cephalothorax, considered, contains, depend, divided, entire, excellent, funnel, funnels, icky, introduction, itsy, poison, practice, practiced, practicing, predator, provides, reason, reasons, scurries, scurry, shiver, shivered, solid, sparkled, spinneret, spinnerets, spinners, spiral, tangle, tangled, valuable, yellow

*__Known Multisyllabic Words With Affixes__ • completed, crackling, deserts, easily, fictional, follows, gardens, hardens, protecting, protection, protects, shelters, spiders, tumbling, wiggling

☆__New Tricky Words__

actually, arachnid, arachnids, breaks, ceiling, ceilings, create, heron, honey, juices, mosquito, obey, obeyed, pour, prey, rhymes, swamps, tarantula, tarantulas, tongues, washed, wasp, wigwam

*__Known Tricky Words With Affixes__ • breaks, certainly, movements, rework

Fluency

Accuracy, Expression, Phrasing, Rate

Vocabulary

__New__ • amphibian, carnivore, cephalothorax, legend, obey, predator, protection, senses, valuable

__Review__ • amazing, carnivore, colony, creature, curious, destroy, fascinating, habit, legend, locate, metamorphosis, permission, protect, protection, reptile, respectful, splendid, vibration

__Reviewed in Context__ • amazed, amazing, colony, creature, destroy, fascinated, fascinating, generation, habitat, locate, metamorphosis, perfect, permission, protect, reptile, splendid, surface, survive, vibration

Comprehension

Unit Genres
Nonfiction • Expository
Fiction • Legend

Comprehension Processes
Build Knowledge: Factual, Procedural, Conceptual

Day	1	2	3	4	5	6	7	8
Remember								
Defining								
Identifying (recalling)	S,C	S,C	S,C	S,C	E,C	C	S,C	S,C
Using	S				E			S
Understand								
Defining (in your own words)	S		S				S	S
Describing			S				S,C	S
Explaining (rephrasing)	S	S	S	S	C		S	S
Illustrating						C		
Sequencing								C
Summarizing	S	S,C	S,C	S,C			S	
Using	S	S,C	S	S,C	C	E	S	S,C
Visualizing						C	S	
Apply								
Demonstrating								S
Explaining (unstated)	S	S		S	C	C	S,C	S
Illustrating								
Inferring	S	S	S	S,C	S		S,C	S
Making Connections (relating)	S		S	S	S			
Predicting					S			S
Using	S,C		S,C	S		E	S	
Analyze								
Classifying	S	C		S				
Comparing/Contrasting	S	S	C					
Distinguishing Cause/Effect								
Drawing Conclusions								
Inferring								
Evaluate								
Making Judgments								
Responding (personal)			S			E		
Create								
Generating Ideas	S		S	S	E,C	E,C	S	S

E = Exercise, S = Storybook, C = Comprehension & Skill

4

Comprehension (continued)

Skills and Strategies

Day	1	2	3	4	5	6	7	8
Priming Background Knowledge	S							
Setting a Purpose for Reading							S	S
Answering Questions	S	S	S	S	S	S	S	S
Asking Questions	S		S	S				
Visualizing						C	S	
Comprehension Monitoring/Fix Ups								
Does it Make Sense?		C		C			E,C	
Looking Back								
Restating								
Summarizing								
Main Idea				C				
Retelling								
Supporting Details	S	S,C	S,C	S,C		C		
Understanding Text Structure								
Title, Author, Illustrator	S	S	S	S	E	S	S	S
Fact or Fiction								
Genre (Classifying)	S						S,C	
Narrative								
Setting							S	S
Main Character/Traits (Characterization)*							S,C*	S
Goal								S
Problem/Solution								S
Action/Events/Sequence								S,C
Outcome/Conclusion						C		
Lesson/Author's Message								
Expository								
Subject/Topic	S,C	S,C		S,C	E,C	C		C
Heading	C	C	C	S,C				
Supporting Details (Facts/Information)	S	S,C	S,C	C	E	C		C
Main Idea				C				C
Using Graphic Organizers								
Chart								
Diagram (labeling)					C			
Hierarchy (topic/detail)				C				
K-W-L	S	S	S	S				
Map (locating, labeling)								
Matrix (compare/contrast)			C					
Sequence (linear, cycle, cause and effect)								
Story Map								
Web								

E = Exercise, S = Storybook, C = Comprehension & Skill

* Narrator

Comprehension (continued)

Study Skills

Day	1	2	3	4	5	6	7	8
Alphabetical Order								
Following Directions								
Locating Information	S,C	C	S	S,C	E	E		
Note Taking	C	C	C	C				C
Previewing								
Reviewing		S	S	S				S
Test Taking							E,C	C
Using Glossary								S
Using Table of Contents	S							
Viewing		S					S	
Verifying	S	S	S	S				

Writing in Response to Reading

Day	1	2	3	4	5	6	7	8
Sentence Completion				C	C	C	C	C
Making Lists								
Sentence Writing				C	C	C		
Story Retell/Summary								
Fact Summary								
Paragraph Writing					C	C	C	
Report Writing					C	C		
Open-Ended Response								
Creative Writing								

Writing Traits

(Addressed within the context of Writing in Response to Reading)

Day	1	2	3	4	5	6	7	8
Ideas and Content								
Elaborating/Generating					C	C		
Organization								
Introduction								
Topic Sentence					C	C		
Supporting Details					C	C		
Sequencing								
Word Choice								
Sophisticated Words (Tier 2 and 3)					C	C	C	
Conventions								
Capital				C	C	C	C	C
Ending Punctuation				C	C	C	C	C
Other (commas, quotation marks)								
Presentation								
Handwriting					C	C	C	C
Neatness					C	C	C	C

E = Exercise, S = Storybook, C = Comprehension & Skill

Daily Lesson Planning

LESSON PLAN FORMAT

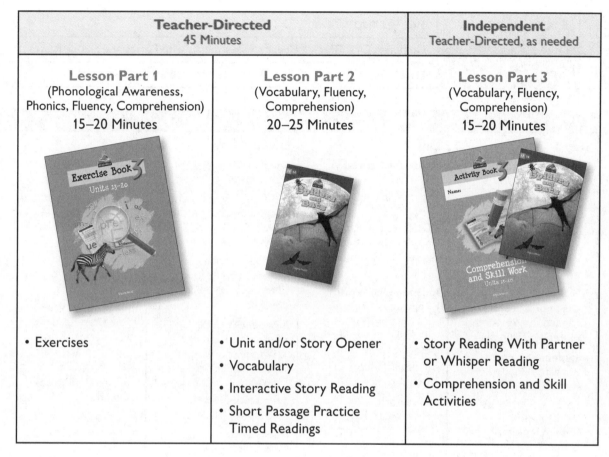

Teacher-Directed 45 Minutes		Independent Teacher-Directed, as needed
Lesson Part 1 (Phonological Awareness, Phonics, Fluency, Comprehension) 15–20 Minutes	**Lesson Part 2** (Vocabulary, Fluency, Comprehension) 20–25 Minutes	**Lesson Part 3** (Vocabulary, Fluency, Comprehension) 15–20 Minutes
• Exercises	• Unit and/or Story Opener • Vocabulary • Interactive Story Reading • Short Passage Practice Timed Readings	• Story Reading With Partner or Whisper Reading • Comprehension and Skill Activities

HOMEWORK

Read Well Homework (blackline masters of new *Read Well 2* passages) provides an opportunity for children to celebrate accomplishments with parents. Homework should be sent home on routine days.

REPORT WRITING

This unit includes a written report activity that begins on Day 5. Look ahead to carefully plan your instructional time.

ORAL READING FLUENCY ASSESSMENT

Upon completion of this unit, assess each student and proceed to Unit 14, as appropriate.

WRITTEN ASSESSMENT

During the time students would normally complete Comprehension and Skill Activities, students will be administered a Written Assessment that can be found on page 99 in the students' *Activity Book 3*.

Note: See Making Decisions for additional assessment information.

---

* The Oral Reading Fluency Assessments are individually administered by the teacher while students are working on their Written Assessments.

† Focus Lesson 7b may be skipped if students are already familiar with Maze Reading.

DIFFERENTIATED LESSON PLANS

The differentiated lesson plans illustrate how to use materials for students with various learning needs. As you set up your unit plan, always include *Read Well 2* Exercises and Story Reading on a daily basis. Unit 13 includes 8-, 9-, 10-, and 11-Day Plans.

Plans	For groups that:
8-DAY	Complete Oral Reading Fluency Assessments with Passes and Strong Passes
9-, 10-, or 11-DAY	Have difficulty passing the unit Oral Reading Fluency Assessments

8-DAY PLAN

Day 1	Day 2	Day 3	Day 4
Teacher-Directed • Exercise 1 • Unit and Story Opener: Spider, Spider, on the Wall • Vocabulary, Ch. 1, 2 • Spider, Spider, on the Wall, Ch. 1 • K-W-L (modified) • Guide practice, as needed, on Research Notes 1, Comp & Skill 1 **Independent Work** • Repeated Reading: Partner or Whisper Read, Spider, Spider, on the Wall, Ch. 1 • Research Notes 1, Comp & Skill 1 **Homework** • Homework Passage 1	**Teacher-Directed** • Exercise 2 • Spider, Spider, on the Wall, Ch. 2 • Guide practice, as needed, on Research Notes 2, Comp & Skill 2 **Independent Work** • Repeated Reading: Partner or Whisper Read, Spider, Spider, on the Wall, Ch. 2 • Research Notes 2, Comp & Skill 2 **Homework** • Homework Passage 2	**Teacher-Directed** • Exercise 3 • Vocabulary, Ch. 3, 4 • Spider, Spider, on the Wall, Ch. 3 • K-W-L (modified) • Guide practice, as needed, on Research Notes 3, Comp & Skill 3 **Independent Work** • Repeated Reading: Partner or Whisper Read, Spider, Spider, on the Wall, Ch. 3 • Research Notes 3, Comp & Skill 3 **Homework** • Homework Passage 3	**Teacher-Directed** • Exercise 4 • Spider, Spider, on the Wall, Ch. 4 • K-W-L (modified) • Guide practice, as needed, on Research Notes 4, Comp & Skill 4 **Independent Work** • Repeated Reading: Partner or Whisper Read, Spider, Spider on the Wall, Ch. 4 • Research Notes 4, Comp & Skill 4 **Homework** • Homework Passage 4

(continued)

Day 5	Day 6	Day 7	Day 8
Teacher-Directed • Exercise 5a • Exercises 5b, 5c: Focus Lessons • Fluency, Fun With Rhymes, Down the Spout Again • Guide practice, as needed, on Report Writing Title Page, Introduction **Independent Work** • Report Writing Title Page, Introduction **Homework** • Homework Passage 5	**Teacher-Directed** • Exercise 6a • Exercises 6b, 6c: Focus Lessons • Guide practice, as needed, on Report Writing Body, Conclusion **Independent Work** • Report Writing Body, Conclusion **Homework** • Homework Passage 6	**Teacher-Directed** • Exercise 7a • Exercise 7b: Focus Lesson† • Story Opener: Centipede and Grandmother Spider • Vocabulary, Intro, Ch. 1 • Centipede and Grandmother Spider, Introduction • Guide practice, as needed, on Comp & Skill Activities 5 and 6 **Independent Work** • On Your Own: Partner or Whisper Read, Centipede and Grandmother Spider, Ch. 1 • Complete Report Writing, Comp & Skill Activities 5 and 6, as time allows **Homework** • Homework Passage 7	**Teacher-Directed** • Exercise 8 • Vocabulary, Ch. 2, 3 • Centipede and Grandmother Spider, Ch. 2 **Independent Work** • On Your Own: Partner or Whisper Read, Centipede and Grandmother Spider, Ch. 3 • Written Assessment • Oral Reading Fluency Assessment* **Homework** • Homework Passage 8

9-, 10-, or 11-DAY PLAN • *Intervention*
For Days 1–8, follow 8-Day plan. Add Days 9, 10, 11 as follows:

Day 9 Extra Practice 1	Day 10 Extra Practice 2	Day 11 Extra Practice 3
Teacher-Directed • Decoding Practice • Fluency Passage **Independent Work** • Activity and Word Fluency A **Homework** • Fluency Passage	**Teacher-Directed** • Decoding Practice • Fluency Passage **Independent Work** • Activity and Word Fluency B **Homework** • Fluency Passage	**Teacher-Directed** • Decoding Practice • Fluency Passage **Independent Work** • Activity and Word Fluency A or B • Oral Reading Fluency Assessment* **Homework** • Fluency Passage

* The Oral Reading Fluency Assessments are individually administered by the teacher while students are working on their Written Assessments.

† Focus Lesson 7b may be skipped if students are already familiar with Maze Reading.

Materials and Materials Preparation

Core Lessons

Teacher Materials

READ WELL 2 MATERIALS

- Unit 13 Teacher's Guide
- Sound Cards
- Unit 13 Oral Reading Fluency Assessment found on page 131
- Group Assessment Record found in the *Assessment Manual*

SCHOOL SUPPLIES

Stopwatch or watch with a second hand

Student Materials

READ WELL 2 MATERIALS (for each student)

- *Spiders and Bats* storybook
- *Exercise Book 3*
- *Activity Book 3* or copies of Unit 13 Comprehension and Skill Work (see Report Writing box at right)
- Unit 13 Written Assessment found in *Activity Book 3*, page 99, and on the blackline master CD
- Unit 13 Certificate of Achievement (BLM, page 132)
- Unit 13 Homework (blackline masters)
  See *Getting Started* for suggested homework routines.

SCHOOL SUPPLIES

Pencils, colors (optional—markers, crayons, or colored pencils)

Make one copy per student of each blackline master, as appropriate for the group. If you're starting the program in Unit 13, make one copy per student of the world map.

Note: For new or difficult Comprehension and Skill Activities, make overhead transparencies from the blackline masters. Use the transparencies to demonstrate and guide practice.

Extra Practice Lessons

CAUTION
Use these lessons only if needed. Students who need Extra Practice may benefit from one, two, or three lessons.

Student Materials

READ WELL 2 MATERIALS (for each student, as needed)

See Extra Practice blackline masters located on the CD.

- Unit 13 Extra Practice 1: Decoding Practice, Fluency Passage, Word Fluency A, and Activity
- Unit 13 Extra Practice 2: Decoding Practice, Fluency Passage, Word Fluency B, and Activity
- Unit 13 Extra Practice 3: Decoding Practice, Fluency Passage, Word Fluency A or B, and Activity

SCHOOL SUPPLIES

Pencils, colors (markers, crayons, or colored pencils), highlighters

REPORT WRITING

For student note-taking, copy and staple Research Notes, Note Taking 1, 2, 3, and 4 together (pages 1–4). Copy and staple the four Report Writing pages as a separate report folder.

FOCUS LESSONS

For Exercises 5b, 5c, 6b, 6c and 7b (Focus Lessons), make overhead transparencies from the blackline masters, write on transparencies placed over the pages, or use paper copies to demonstrate how to complete the lessons.

Important Tips

Expectations and Adaptations for Written Work, Report Writing

EXPECTATIONS

Teach and reteach written work expectations.

Explain expectations and verify students' understanding.

1. **Keep your paper flat, whole, and neat.**
   What should your paper look like? (flat, whole, and neat)
2. **Your next job is to write as neatly as you can.**
3. **Provide negative and positive examples, as needed.**
4. **Provide gentle, supportive corrections.**
5. **Acknowledge students' accomplishments and efforts.**
   Provide each student with a sample of his or her own personal best to use as a reference.

ADAPTATIONS

Reminder: If you are working with low-performing students, your highest priority is to move them forward as rapidly as possible with fluency and understanding. Do not hold students back due to their inability to complete written work. These difficulties may be due to lack of fine motor skills, handwriting fluency, and spelling.

If a student or students lack fine motor skills, handwriting fluency, and/or reasonable spelling skills, adapt the written assignments. Consider the following procedures:

1. Do group note taking. Have the group orally dictate notes for Comprehension and Skill Research Notes, Notetaking 1, 2, 3, and 4 (pages 1–4 in *Activity Book 3*). Write the notes on an overhead or enlarged copy of the activity. Have students copy the notes.

2. Have the group orally generate each part of the report (Comprehension and Skill Report Writing, pages 9–12 in *Activity Book 3*). Write each part of the report in nice handwriting for students. Make a copy of each completed page for students. Have students trace the report in their best handwriting the next day. (You may wish to let students use fine-tip marker pens as an added incentive to copy neatly.)

3. Work on handwriting fluency on a daily basis.
   • Have students trace or copy the alphabet.
   • Have students trace and then copy the same sentence a couple of times.
   • Have students copy passages from the story.
   • Have students copy or trace responses that have been orally dictated.

> Post this poem on a bulletin board and have students read it periodically.
>
> I'll put myself to the test.
> I'll do my very best.
>
> I'll keep my paper flat.
> I'll do it just like that.
>
> I'll keep my paper whole.
> Oh, what a goal!
>
> I'll keep my paper neat.
> My writing can't be beat.
>
> I'll put myself to the test.
> I'll always do my best.

> If you expect it, you must teach it, acknowledge each students' personal best, and reteach periodically.

How to Teach the Lessons

Teach from this section. Each instructional component is outlined in an easy-to-teach format.

Exercise 1

- Unit and Story Opener: Spiders;
  Spider, Spider, on the Wall
- Vocabulary
- Story Reading 1
  With the Teacher: Chapter 1
- Research Notes 1, Comprehension and Skill
  Activity 1

Exercise 2

- Story Reading 2
  With the Teacher: Chapter 2
- Research Notes 2, Comprehension and
  Skill Activity 2

Exercise 3

- Vocabulary
- Story Reading 3
  With the Teacher: Chapter 3
- Research Notes 3, Comprehension and Skill Activity 3

Exercise 4

- Story Reading 4
  With the Teacher: Chapter 4
- Research Notes 4, Comprehension and Skill Activity 4

Exercise 5a

- Exercise 5b: Focus Lesson
- Exercise 5c: Focus Lesson
- Story Reading 5
  With the Teacher: Fun With Rhymes,
  Down the Spout Again (Fluency)
- Report Writing Title Page, Introduction

Note: Lessons include daily homework.

Exercise 6a

- Exercise 6b: Focus Lesson
- Exercise 6c: Focus Lesson
- Report Writing Body, Conclusion

Exercise 7a

- Exercise 7b: Focus Lesson
- Story Opener: Centipede and Grandmother Spider
- Vocabulary
- Story Reading 6
  With the Teacher: Introduction
  On Your Own: Chapter 1
- Complete Report Writing, Comprehension and
  Skill Activities 5 and 6, as time allows

Exercise 8

- Vocabulary
- Story Reading 7
  With the Teacher: Chapter 2
  On Your Own: Chapter 3
- Written Assessment

❶ SOUND REVIEW

Use selected Sound Cards from Units 1–12.

PACING

Exercise 1 should take about 15 minutes.

★ ❷ NEW SOUND INTRODUCTION

- For Row A, tell students they will learn the sound for <u>o-y</u>.
  Say something like:
  Look at the picture. Say "<u>o-y</u> says /oy/ as in boy." (<u>o-y</u> says /oy/ as in boy)
  Read the sentences. (Look at the joy on Roy's face. He is a happy boy with a new toy.)
  Which four words have the /oy/ sound? (joy, Roy's, boy, toy)

- For Row B, have students read the underlined sound, then the word.
- After reading the row, have students go back and read the whole words.

❸ ACCURACY AND FLUENCY BUILDING

- For each task, have students say any underlined part, then read the word.
- Set a pace. Then have students read the whole words in each task and column.
- Provide repeated practice, building accuracy first, then fluency.

E1. Tricky Words

- For each Tricky Word, have students use the sounds and word parts they know to silently sound out the word. Use the word in a sentence to help with pronunciation.
- If the word is unfamiliar, tell students the word.

tongues
Look at the first word. The word is *tongues*.
People taste food with their . . . *tongues*. Read the word two times. (tongues, tongues)

actually   A spider is not an insect. It is . . . *actually* . . . an arachnid.

therefore
Look at the next word. You know the first part. Try and figure out the word by parts.
Thumbs up when you know the word. What's the word? (therefore)
I want to learn . . . *therefore* . . . *I read.* Read the word two times. (therefore, therefore)

group   The band members gathered in a . . . *group.*
movements   The hummingbird made rapid . . . *movements.*
although   I am doing my math homework . . . *although* . . . it's not due until next week.

- Have students go back and read the whole words in the column.

❹ MULTISYLLABIC WORDS

For each word, have students read the syllables, then the whole word. Use the word in a sentence, as appropriate.

arachnids   Spiders are not insects. They are . . . *arachnids.*
vibrations   Earthworms can feel . . . *vibrations.*
ability   He is a great gymnast. He has the . . . *ability* . . . to do flips.
contains   The glass . . . *contains* . . . water.
spinnerets   Spiders spin silk with . . . *spinnerets.*
cephalothorax   The part of a spider's body that has the head and chest is the . . . *cephalothorax.*

⑤ GENERALIZATION: READING NEW WORDS IN PARAGRAPHS

- Have students read the paragraph silently, then out loud. Tell students to use the sounds and word parts they know to read any difficult words.
- Repeat practice, as needed.

Spider, Spider, On the Wall

Unit 13 Exercise 1
Use before Chapter 1

1. SOUND REVIEW Use selected Sound Cards from Units 1–12.

★2. NEW SOUND INTRODUCTION Introduce the new sound /oy/ as in boy.

Ⓐ		
oy	boy	Look at the joy on Roy's face. He is a happy boy with a new toy.

Ⓑ	soy	enjoy	annoy	employ

3. ACCURACY/FLUENCY BUILDING For each column, have students say any underlined part, then read each word. Next, have them read the column.

A1 Mixed Practice	**B1** Bossy E	**C1** Morphographs & Affixes	**D1** Word Endings	**E1** Tricky Words
protect	plates	depend	senses	tongues
types	bites	belong	gardens	actually
deserts	survive	unlike	smelling	therefore
liquid	divided	protection	smartest	group
poison		excellent		movements
peep	taste		body	although
chest	tasting		bodies	

4. MULTISYLLABIC WORDS Have students read each word part, then read each whole word.

Ⓐ	ar•ach•nids	arachnids	vi•bra•tions	vibrations
Ⓑ	a•bil•i•ty	ability	con•tains	contains
Ⓒ	spin•ner•ets	spinnerets	ceph•a•lo•thor•ax	cephalothorax

5. GENERALIZATION Have students read the paragraph silently, then out loud. (New words: ceiling, creep, fangs, ability)

Meg saw a big spider run across the ceiling and down the wall. Meg loved spiders! She tried to quietly creep up on it so she could study it more closely. The eight-legged creature had a beautiful yellow and black abdomen. It was so large that Meg could even see its fangs. "Wow!" thought Meg. "I wish I could catch that spider. Then I could take it to school."

GENERALIZATION
(Reminder)

The generalization task provides an opportunity for you to informally assess students' ability to read new words that have not been pretaught.

1

COMPREHENSION PROCESSES

Remember, Understand, Apply

PROCEDURES

1. **Introducing the Storybook**

   Identifying—Title; Inferring—Topic
   Have students identify the title of their new storybook.
   Say something like:
   Everyone, look at the cover of your new storybook.
   What's the title of your new storybook? (Spiders and Bats)

   What is this storybook about? (spiders and bats)
   That's right. Look at the picture.

2. **Introducing the Unit and Story**

   Using the Table of Contents; Identifying—Titles; Inferring; Classifying—Genre; Explaining
   Have students find the Table of Contents and identify the name of their new unit and story.
   Say something like:
   Everyone, find the Table of Contents.
   What's the title of our new unit?
   (Spiders)
   What's the title of our new story?
   (Spider, Spider, on the Wall)

   That's right. "Spider, Spider, on the Wall" is nonfiction. What does that mean? (It's true.)

   Next, we're going to read "Fun with Rhymes."

   Then this storybook ends with "Centipede and Grandmother Spider." Do you think this story will be fact or fiction? (fiction)

   How can you tell?
   (Grandmother Spider sounds like a make-believe character.)
   Right! We don't usually call spiders grandmothers.

2

3. Using K-W-L (modified)

Using Graphic Organizer, Priming Background Knowledge, Asking Questions

- Use chart paper or three columns on a chalkboard to make a K-W-L chart.

- Demonstrate and explain that it's okay to make corrections in our knowledge. Then have students identify what they think they know about spiders. Say something like:

  Remember, sometimes we learn new facts that make us change the way we think about things. Here is a fact that I think I know about spiders.

  I think all spiders spin webs.

  I'm going to write that on the board.

  Note: "All spiders spin webs" is incorrect. Students will enjoy correcting that fact to "Most spiders spin webs" after reading page 24 in the storybook.

  What do you think you already know about spiders?

  (Spiders have eight legs. Spiders are small. Spiders bite . . .)

K-W-L (modified)

Spiders

What do we think we <u>k</u>now?	What do we <u>w</u>ant to know?	What did we <u>l</u>earn?
All spiders spin webs (Ms. M)	Where do spiders live? (Ms. M)	
8 legs (Lee)	Are they dangerous? (Lee)	
Make webs (Andrea)	Are they herbivores, carnivores, or omnivores? (Jay)	
Small (Colleen)		
Bite (Pedro)		

- Think aloud as you demonstrate how to ask questions. Then have students generate questions about spiders. Say something like:

  I wonder where spiders live. I think they live in many different places. My question is "Where do spiders live?"

COMPREHENSION PROCESSES

Remember, Understand, Apply

PROCEDURES

Introducing Vocabulary

> ☆ **cephalothorax** ☆ **senses,**
> **vibration, protect**
> ☆ **protection**

- For each vocabulary word, have students read the word by parts, then read the whole word.
- Read the student-friendly explanations to students as they follow with their fingers. Then have students use the vocabulary word by following the gray text.
- Review and discuss the photos.

USING VOCABULARY

WITH THE TEACHER

Chapters 1, 2

Vocabulary

★ **ceph·a·lo·thor·ax**

The **cephalothorax** is the body part of a spider that contains the head and chest.

A spider has two body parts, a *cephalothorax* and an abdomen. Look at the picture. Touch the cephalothorax of the spider. What did you touch?[1]

★ **sens·es**

People and animals have **senses** that tell them about things around them. The five senses are the ability to see, hear, smell, taste, and touch.

Dogs have a great *sense* of smell. What can dogs do because of their great sense of smell?[2]

vi·bra·tion

A **vibration** is a shaking movement that you can feel.

I could feel the *vibration* from the jackhammer. Can you imagine how it would feel to hold a jackhammer?[3]

★ = New

8

---

❶ Understand: Using Vocabulary—cephalothorax (I touched the cephalothorax of the spider.)

❷ Apply: Using Vocabulary—senses (Dogs can smell things that people can't smell. A dog's great sense of smell means that it can hunt other animals and find missing people.)

❸ Apply: Making Connections; Using Vocabulary—vibration, imagine (It would be awesome. The vibration would make my hands and body shake.)

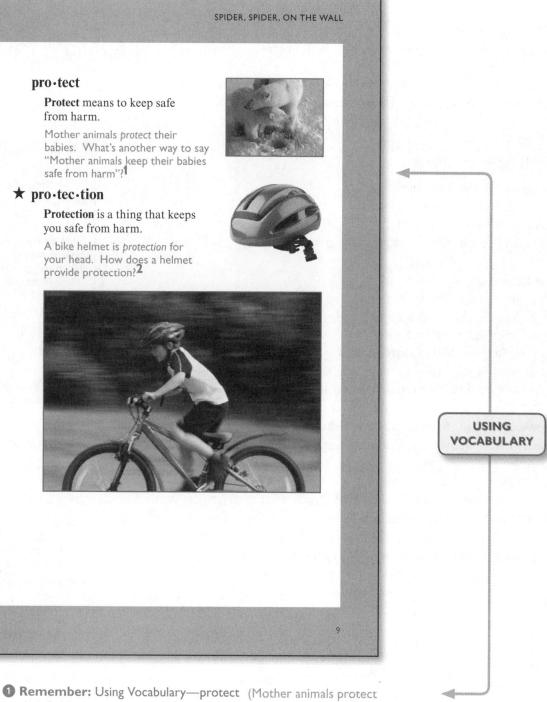

SPIDER, SPIDER, ON THE WALL

pro·tect

Protect means to keep safe from harm.

Mother animals *protect* their babies. What's another way to say "Mother animals keep their babies safe from harm"?[1]

★ **pro·tec·tion**

Protection is a thing that keeps you safe from harm.

A bike helmet is *protection* for your head. How does a helmet provide protection?[2]

9

USING VOCABULARY

❶ **Remember:** Using Vocabulary—protect (Mother animals protect their babies.)

❷ **Apply:** Explaining; **Understand:** Defining Vocabulary—protection (A helmet covers your head so your head won't get hurt if you have an accident.)

CHAPTER 1 INSTRUCTIONS
Students read Chapter 1 with the teacher.

COMPREHENSION PROCESSES
Remember, Understand, Apply, Analyze, Create

COMPREHENSION BUILDING
- Encourage students to answer questions with complete sentences, when appropriate.
- If students have difficulty comprehending, think aloud with them or reread the portion of the story that answers the question. Repeat the question.

PROCEDURES

1. Introducing the Chapter

Identifying—Title; Inferring

Discuss the title and main characters. Say something like:

What's the title of this chapter? (An Eight-Legged Creature)

What is the eight-legged creature we're going to learn about?

2. First Reading
- Ask questions and discuss the text as indicated by the gray text.
- Mix group and individual turns, independent of your voice. Have students work toward a group accuracy goal of 0–5 errors. Quietly keep track of errors made by all students in the group.
- After reading the story, practice any difficult words. Repeat, if students have not reached the accuracy goal.

3. Second Reading, Short Passage Practice: Developing Prosody
- Demonstrate expressive, fluent reading of the first paragraph. Read at a rate slightly faster than the students' rate.
- Guide practice with your voice.
- Provide individual turns while others track with their fingers and whisper read.
- Repeat with one paragraph at a time.

4. Partner or Whisper Reading: Repeated Reading
 Before beginning independent work, have students finger track and partner or whisper read.

5. Comprehension and Skill Work
Tell students they will do Research Notes (Note Taking 1) and Comprehension and Skill Activity 1 after they read Chapter 1. Guide practice, as needed. For teacher directions, see pages 27 and 28. Tell students to save their Research Notes because they will need them for report writing.

6. Homework 1: Repeated Reading

> ### REPEATED READINGS
> **Prosody**
> On the second reading, students practice developing prosody— phrasing and expression. Research has shown that prosody is related to both fluency and comprehension.

> ### CORRECTING DECODING ERRORS
> During story reading, gently correct any error, then have students reread the sentence.

WITH THE TEACHER

Chapter 1

An Eight-Legged Creature

Spider Parts

Did you know that spiders are not insects? Insects have six legs and three body parts. Spiders have eight legs and two body parts. Most insects have wings, but spiders never have wings. Spiders belong to a group of animals called arachnids.

Look at the pictures. Count the body parts on the spider and the insect. How are they different? ¹Count the legs on the spider and the insect. How are they different? ²A spider isn't an insect. It's an . . . ³

10

COMPREHENDING
AS YOU GO

❶ **Analyze:** Contrasting (The spider has two body parts, and the insect has three body parts.)

❷ **Analyze:** Contrasting (The spider has eight legs, and the insect has six legs.)

❸ **Remember:** Identifying—What (arachnid)

Types of Spiders

There are about 40,000 different types of spiders. Some are as tiny as the dot on the letter i. Others are as big as dinner plates. Spiders come in many colors and live in many places. You can find them in gardens, forests, deserts, mountains, and even your own home. Unlike ants, spiders do not live in colonies. They live alone. But like ants, they need other living things to survive.

Name some facts about spiders from this last paragraph.[1]

11

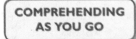

COMPREHENDING
AS YOU GO

1 **Understand:** Summarizing—Facts (There are 40,000 different kinds of spiders. Spiders come in many colors and live in many places. Some spiders are as big as dinner plates . . .)

WITH THE TEACHER

Spider Anatomy

    A spider's body is divided into two parts. The front part is the cephalothorax—the head and chest. The bigger part is the abdomen.

    All spiders have eight legs. Their legs actually come out of their heads! They can walk up walls and across ceilings because they have special grip pads on their feet.

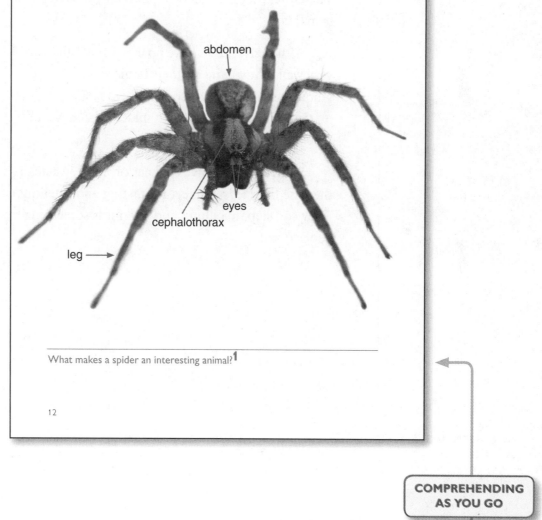

What makes a spider an interesting animal?[1]

12

COMPREHENDING
AS YOU GO

❶ Remember: Identifying—What; **Understand:** Summarizing—Facts (A spider is interesting because its legs come out of its head, and it can walk up walls . . .)

SPIDER, SPIDER, ON THE WALL

All spiders have long sharp teeth called fangs. Spider fangs have poison in them. Spiders bite to kill things to eat. Don't worry—very few spider bites hurt people.

Spider Senses

Spiders have lots of eyes—sometimes as many as eight. Even so, most spiders can't see very well. Therefore, they must depend on their other senses to help them.

Although spiders have no ears, they can hear very well. Tiny hairs on their bodies pick up sound vibrations. The hairs also help them feel movements on the ground and in water. Spiders also have an excellent sense of touch.

Spiders do not have tongues or noses. Instead, they use their legs and feet for tasting and smelling. They can step in a liquid and tell if it is something good to eat!

Do spiders have ears?[1] How do they hear?[2] Do spiders have tongues or noses?[3] How do they taste?[4] Can spiders see well?[5] What *sense* do they depend on the most?[6]

13

COMPREHENDING AS YOU GO

[1] **Remember:** Identifying—Fact (No, spiders do not have ears.)

[2] **Understand:** Explaining; Using Vocabulary—vibrations (Tiny hairs on their bodies pick up the vibrations made by sound.)

[3] **Remember:** Identifying—Fact (No, spiders do not have tongues or noses.)

[4] **Understand:** Explaining (Spiders use their legs and feet for tasting.)

[5] **Remember:** Identifying—Fact (No, spiders can't see very well.)

[6] **Understand:** Explaining; Using Vocabulary—senses (Spiders depend on their sense of hearing.)

WITH THE TEACHER

Spider, Spider, on the wall,
Are you the smartest of them all?
With eight legs to crawl and creep,
You have no ears to hear a peep.
Yet when it's food you need,
Your sense of touch will help you feed.
Spider, Spider, on the wall,
Indeed, you are a know-it-all!

14

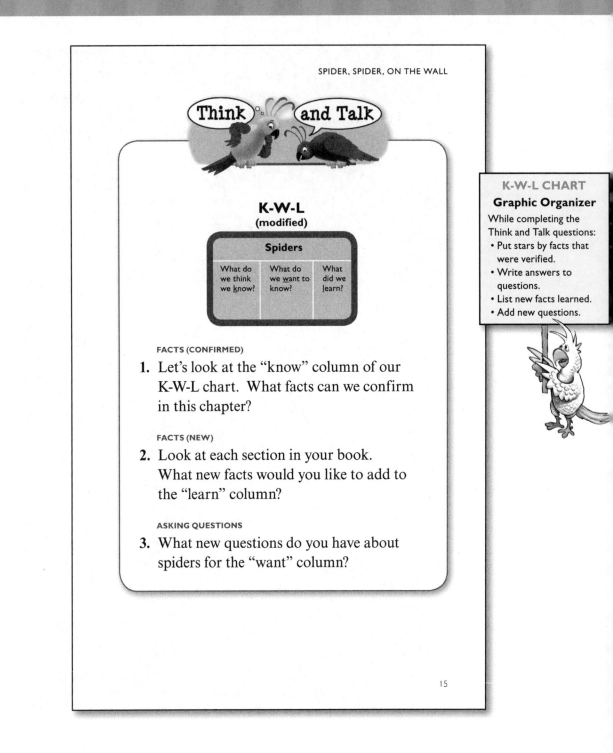

SPIDER, SPIDER, ON THE WALL

Think and Talk

K-W-L
(modified)

Spiders

What do we think we <u>k</u>now?	What do we <u>w</u>ant to know?	What did we <u>l</u>earn?

K-W-L CHART
Graphic Organizer
While completing the Think and Talk questions:
• Put stars by facts that were verified.
• Write answers to questions.
• List new facts learned.
• Add new questions.

FACTS (CONFIRMED)

1. Let's look at the "know" column of our K-W-L chart. What facts can we confirm in this chapter?

FACTS (NEW)

2. Look at each section in your book. What new facts would you like to add to the "learn" column?

ASKING QUESTIONS

3. What new questions do you have about spiders for the "want" column?

15

❶ **Apply:** Locating Information; Verifying—Facts (Spiders are arachnids. Spiders have eight legs.)

❷ **Understand:** Locating Information; Summarizing—Facts; Using Vocabulary—colony (Spiders have two body parts. Spiders never have wings. There are 40,000 different types of spiders. Spiders live in many places, and they live alone, not in colonies. Spiders' legs come out of their heads. They have grip pads on their feet. Few spider bites hurt people. Spiders have lots of eyes, but no ears, tongues, or noses.)

❸ **Create:** Generating Ideas, Asking Questions (Do spiders sleep? Do spiders lay eggs?)

NOTE TAKING 1 • LOCATING INFORMATION

COMPREHENSION PROCESSES

Remember, Understand

Identifying—Topic; Using Headings;
Summarizing—Facts

PROCEDURES

For each step, demonstrate and guide practice, as needed. Then have students complete the page independently.

SPECIAL NOTE

- On Days 1–4, your students will take notes. For ease of use, pull Research Notes 1–4 out and staple them together.
- On Days 5 and 6, students will use their notes to write a report. Pull out Report Writing to create report folders.

Note Taking: Locating Information—Specific Instructions

- Have students read the instructions.
Read the instructions. (In this unit you will take research notes and write your own report. Very cool . . .)

The first topic is done for us. Look at the example. What's the topic? (Spider Parts)

The facts in the example are from your storybook. Read the facts.
(eight legs, two body parts, not insects, arachnids)

Spider, Spider, on the Wall

Unit 13 Research Notes   Use with Exercise 1 and Chapter 1

Teachers: If you are using the Activity Book, tear out and staple pages 1–4 to make a Research Notes folder.

Name _____

Note Taking 1

Locating Information
An Eight-Legged Creature

In this unit, you will take research notes and write your own report. Very cool! You will take notes on topics that you think are interesting. The first one has been done for you. Look in your storybook on page 10. The first topic is Spider Parts. Can you find the facts in this section of your storybook?

Topic: Spider Parts *heading*

Fact 1: eight legs

Fact 2: two body parts

Fact 3: not insects, arachnids

There are three more topics in this chapter. Select two topics that you think are interesting, and write three facts about each topic. Write down facts that you think are interesting.
(Accept any reasonable response.)

Topic: Types of Spiders

Fact 1: 40,000 different kinds

Fact 2: many colors

Fact 3: live alone

Topic: Spider Senses

Fact 1: hairs to hear with

Fact 2: excellent sense of touch

Fact 3: legs and feet used for tasting

Save your notes for your report!

©2009 Sopris West Educational Services. All Rights Reserved.   1

Turn to page 10 of your storybook. Point to the first heading. What does it say? (Spider Parts)
Find the sentence that tells us spiders have eight legs. Read the sentence.
(Spiders have eight legs and two body parts.)
Great. That sentence has two of the important facts listed in the note-taking example.

Fact 3 in our research notes says "not insects, arachnids." The paragraph doesn't say "Spiders aren't insects." Instead it asks, "Did you know that spiders are not insects?"
That's another way to state the fact. Read the last sentence of the paragraph.
(Spiders belong to a group of animals called arachnids.) That's the last fact in the notes.

- Have students read the next set of instructions and locate two more topics that they think are interesting. Then have students write the topic in the blanks and write three facts of their choice. Say something like:
Read the next set of instructions. (There are three more topics in this chapter. Select . . .)
Look in the storybook. There are three more topics. What are the topics? (Types of Spiders . . .)
On your Comp and Skill, choose two topics and then list three interesting facts for each.

- Have students save this activity for a report they will write later.

PASSAGE READING FLUENCY

FLUENCY

Accuracy, Expression, Rate

PROCEDURES

For each step, demonstrate and guide practice, as needed. Then have students complete the page independently.

Passage Reading—Basic Instructions

- Have students read the practice words.
- Have students finger track and whisper read the story two times—the first time for accuracy and the second time for expression. Have students cross out a spider each time they finish.
- Have students do a one-minute Timed Reading and cross out the timer.

  You are going to track with your finger and whisper read.

  Read the passage three times. The first time, read for accuracy.

  What will you read for? (accuracy)

  The second time, read for accuracy and expression. What will you read for? (accuracy and expression)

  Each time you read, cross out a spider and notice how much better your reading sounds.

  The last time you read, use the timer. Read quickly but accurately and with expression.

  See if you can finish reading before one minute is up.

> **ACCURACY PRECEDES RATE**
> **(Reminder)**
>
> Students should read the story with a high degree of accuracy before proceeding to Timed Readings. Reading for increased rate before establishing a high degree of accuracy may encourage students to guess at words.

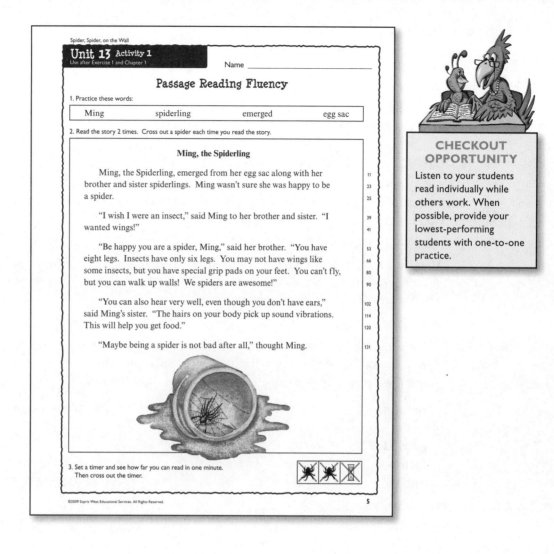

Spider, Spider, on the Wall

Unit 13 Activity 1
Use after Exercise 1 and Chapter 1

Name _____

Passage Reading Fluency

1. Practice these words:

| Ming | spiderling | emerged | egg sac |

2. Read the story 2 times. Cross out a spider each time you read the story.

Ming, the Spiderling

Ming, the Spiderling, emerged from her egg sac along with her brother and sister spiderlings. Ming wasn't sure she was happy to be a spider. — 11 23 25

"I wish I were an insect," said Ming to her brother and sister. "I wanted wings!" — 39 41

"Be happy you are a spider, Ming," said her brother. "You have eight legs. Insects have only six legs. You may not have wings like some insects, but you have special grip pads on your feet. You can't fly, but you can walk up walls! We spiders are awesome!" — 53 66 80 90

"You can also hear very well, even though you don't have ears," said Ming's sister. "The hairs on your body pick up sound vibrations. This will help you get food." — 102 114 120

"Maybe being a spider is not bad after all," thought Ming. — 131

3. Set a timer and see how far you can read in one minute. Then cross out the timer.

5

CHECKOUT OPPORTUNITY

Listen to your students read individually while others work. When possible, provide your lowest-performing students with one-to-one practice.

❶ SOUND REVIEW
Use selected Sound Cards from Units 1–13.

❷ SHIFTY WORD BLENDING
For each word, have students say the underlined sound. Then have them sound out the word smoothly and say it. Use the words in sentences, as appropriate.

❸ ACCURACY AND FLUENCY BUILDING
- For each task, have students say any underlined part, then read the word.
- Set a pace. Then have students read the whole words in each task and column.
- Provide repeated practice, building accuracy first, then fluency.

B2. Compound Words
Have students tell you what a compound word is. Then have them read the words.
A compound word is made of two . . . (small words). Yes, a compound word is made of two small words. Read the compound words.

C1. Multisyllabic Words
- For the list of words divided by syllables, have students read each syllable, then the whole word. Use the word in a sentence, as appropriate.
- For the list of whole words, build accuracy, then fluency.

reasons	I wanted to know why we couldn't use the computer. I wanted to know the . . . *reasons*.
provides	A house . . . *provides* . . . shelter.
follows	My dog goes where I go. He . . . *follows* . . . me everywhere.
entire	I read the whole book. I read the . . . *entire* . . . thing.

E1. Tricky Words
- For each Tricky Word, have students use the sounds and word parts they know to silently sound out the word. Use the word in a sentence to help with pronunciation.
- If the word is unfamiliar, tell students the word.

climb	The hike up the mountain was a long . . . *climb*.
usually	On most days, Juanita gets up at six. She . . . *usually* . . . gets up at six.
pushes	When Mom goes to the market, she gets a shopping cart and . . . *pushes* . . . it.
wonder	Geoffrey looked at the falling star with . . . *wonder*.

❹ MULTISYLLABIC WORDS
For each word, have students read the syllables, then the whole word. Use the word in a sentence, as appropriate.

thickness	The wood was an inch thick. That was its . . . *thickness*.
insects	Flies are . . . *insects*.
hardens	When clay dries, it . . . *hardens*.
hungry	My stomach was growling because I was . . . *hungry*.
abdomen	Spiders have two body parts. They have a head and an . . . *abdomen*.
stronger	Mom always tells me to eat well so that I will get . . . *stronger*.

⭐ = New in this unit

⑤ MORPHOGRAPHS AND AFFIXES

★Have students practice reading *-ous* and the related words. Use each word in a sentence.
- For Row B, have students read the underlined part, then the word.
- For the word "rebuild," review the meaning of the morphograph.
- Repeat practice with whole words, mixing group and individual turns.

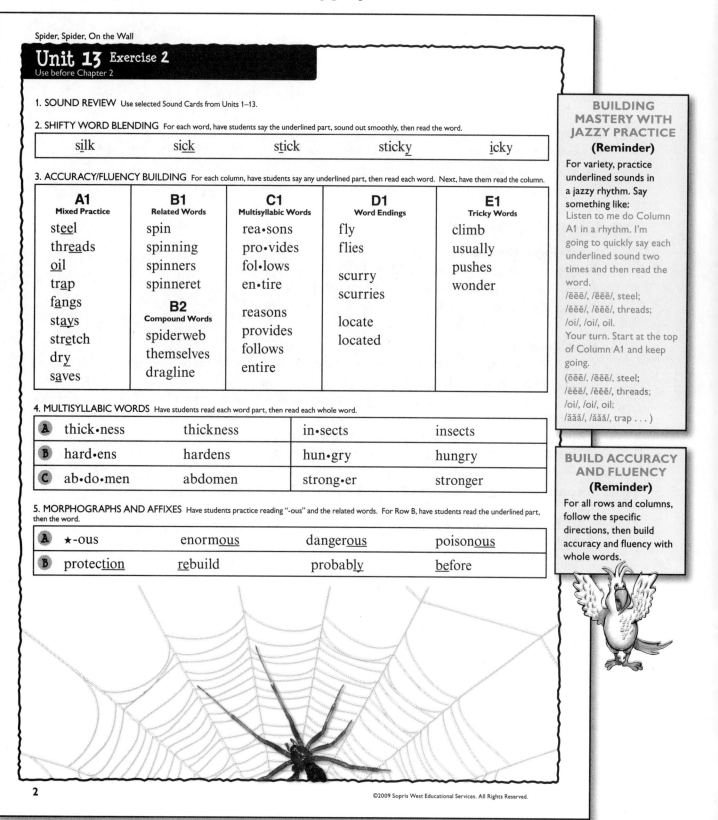

Spider, Spider, On the Wall

Unit 13 Exercise 2
Use before Chapter 2

1. SOUND REVIEW Use selected Sound Cards from Units 1–13.

2. SHIFTY WORD BLENDING For each word, have students say the underlined part, sound out smoothly, then read the word.

| s<u>i</u>lk | si<u>ck</u> | s<u>t</u>ick | stick<u>y</u> | <u>icky</u> |

3. ACCURACY/FLUENCY BUILDING For each column, have students say any underlined part, then read each word. Next, have them read the column.

A1 Mixed Practice	B1 Related Words	C1 Multisyllabic Words	D1 Word Endings	E1 Tricky Words
st<u>ee</u>l	spin	rea•sons	fly	climb
thr<u>ea</u>ds	spinning	pro•vides	flies	usually
<u>oi</u>l	spinners	fol•lows		pushes
tr<u>a</u>p	spinneret	en•tire	scurry	wonder
f<u>a</u>ngs	**B2** Compound Words		scurries	
st<u>ays</u>	spiderweb	reasons		
stre<u>tch</u>	themselves	provides	locate	
dr<u>y</u>	dragline	follows	located	
s<u>a</u>ves		entire		

4. MULTISYLLABIC WORDS Have students read each word part, then read each whole word.

Ⓐ	thick•ness	thickness	in•sects	insects
Ⓑ	hard•ens	hardens	hun•gry	hungry
Ⓒ	ab•do•men	abdomen	strong•er	stronger

5. MORPHOGRAPHS AND AFFIXES Have students practice reading "-ous" and the related words. For Row B, have students read the underlined part, then the word.

Ⓐ	★-ous	enorm<u>ous</u>	danger<u>ous</u>	poison<u>ous</u>
Ⓑ	protec<u>tion</u>	<u>re</u>build	proba<u>bly</u>	<u>be</u>fore

---

BUILDING MASTERY WITH JAZZY PRACTICE
(Reminder)

For variety, practice underlined sounds in a jazzy rhythm. Say something like:
Listen to me do Column A1 in a rhythm. I'm going to quickly say each underlined sound two times and then read the word.
/ēēē/, /ēēē/, steel;
/ĕĕĕ/, /ĕĕĕ/, threads;
/oi/, /oi/, oil.
Your turn. Start at the top of Column A1 and keep going.
(/ēēē/, /ēēē/, steel;
/ĕĕĕ/, /ĕĕĕ/, threads;
/oi/, /oi/, oil;
/ăăă/, /ăăă/, trap . . .)

BUILD ACCURACY AND FLUENCY
(Reminder)

For all rows and columns, follow the specific directions, then build accuracy and fluency with whole words.

CHAPTER 2 INSTRUCTIONS

Students read Chapter 2 with the teacher.

COMPREHENSION PROCESSES

Remember, Understand, Apply

PROCEDURES

1. Reviewing Chapter 1

Summarizing—Facts

Have students turn to page 10. Quickly review some of the facts learned in Chapter 1.
Say something like:

Let's see what we remember from yesterday.

How is a spider different from an insect? (A spider has eight legs, and an insect has six . . .)

Do spiders have ears or noses? (no)

What sense do spiders depend on the most? (Their sense of hearing.)

2. Introducing Chapter 2

Identifying—Title; Inferring

Discuss the title. Say something like:

What's the title of this chapter? (Icky, Sticky Webs)

What do you think we will be reading about? (spiderwebs)

3. First Reading

- Ask questions and discuss the story as indicated by the gray text.
- Mix group and individual turns, independent of your voice.
  Have students work toward a group accuracy goal of 0–6 errors.
  Quietly keep track of errors made by all students in the group.
- After reading the story, practice any difficult words.
  Reread the story if students have not reached the accuracy goal.

4. Second Reading, Timed Readings: Repeated Reading

- As time allows, have students do Timed Readings while others follow along.
- Time individuals for 30 seconds and encourage each child to work for a personal best.
- Determine words correct per minute. Record student scores.

5. Partner or Whisper Reading: Repeated Reading

Before beginning independent work, have students finger track and partner or whisper read.

6. Comprehension and Skill Work

Tell students they will do Research Notes (Note Taking 2) and Comprehension and Skill Activity 2 after they read Chapter 2. Guide practice, as needed. For teacher directions, see pages 38 and 39. Remind students to save their Research Notes for report writing.

7. Homework 2: Repeated Reading

WITH THE TEACHER

Chapter 2

Icky, Sticky Webs

Have you ever walked through the garden and run into the icky, sticky threads of a spiderweb? A spider probably just made that web the night before. In fact, spinning a web is one of the most amazing things that spiders do.

Silk Spinners

Most spiders spin webs. The webs are made from silk that is made by a spinneret. The spinnerets are located under the spider, toward the rear of its abdomen. The silk in the spinnerets is liquid. As soon as the spider pushes the silk out of its body, the liquid silk hardens into a strong thread. This silk thread is up to five times stronger than steel thread of the same thickness.

The silk threads are very, very thin. If you could put all the silk threads from a spider's web from end to end, they would stretch out for hundreds of feet. If you took those same threads and rolled them into a ball, the ball would be no bigger than a grain of rice!

How do spiders make silk?[1] What's special about the silk threads?[2]
Look at the picture on page 17. Find the spinnerets. Why aren't we able to see a spider's spinnerets?[3]

16

REVISING THE K-W-L CHART

Graphic Organizer

After completing the page, say something like:

Look at the first sentence under "Silk Spinners." It says, "*Most* spiders spin webs." That's interesting. I thought *all* spiders spin webs. Let's fix that on our K-W-L chart. It's fun to learn new information. We are becoming spider experts!

Revise the K-W-L chart to reflect new knowledge.

COMPREHENDING AS YOU GO

❶ **Understand:** Explaining (Spiders push silk out of their spinnerets. When the silk leaves the spider's body, it hardens into a strong thread.)

❷ **Understand:** Explaining (The silk threads are very thin and very strong. The thread is stronger than steel thread of the same thickness.)

❸ **Apply:** Viewing, Inferring (The spinnerets are too small.)

SPIDER, SPIDER, ON THE WALL

spinnerets

17

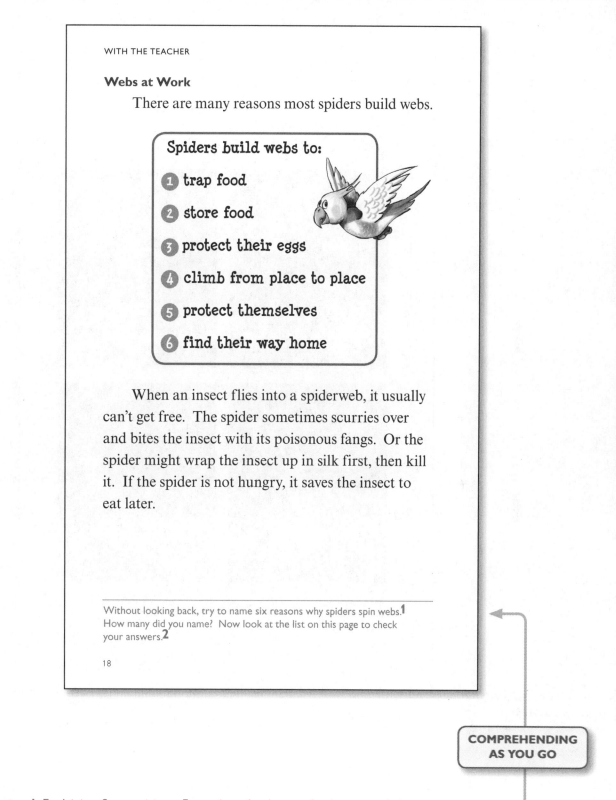

WITH THE TEACHER

Webs at Work

There are many reasons most spiders build webs.

Spiders build webs to:

1 trap food

2 store food

3 protect their eggs

4 climb from place to place

5 protect themselves

6 find their way home

When an insect flies into a spiderweb, it usually can't get free. The spider sometimes scurries over and bites the insect with its poisonous fangs. Or the spider might wrap the insect up in silk first, then kill it. If the spider is not hungry, it saves the insect to eat later.

Without looking back, try to name six reasons why spiders spin webs.**1** How many did you name? Now look at the list on this page to check your answers.**2**

18

COMPREHENDING AS YOU GO

1 Understand: Explaining; Summarizing—Facts (trap food, store food, protect their eggs, climb from place to place, protect themselves, find their way home)

2 Apply: Verifying—Facts

Spiders also use silk to wrap and protect their eggs. The entire silk web provides protection for the spider. The web traps insects and small birds that want to eat the spider.

Look at the picture and explain what happens to an insect that flies into a spider's web.¹

19

**COMPREHENDING
AS YOU GO**

❶ **Understand:** Viewing; **Apply:** Explaining (An insect that flies into a spiderweb usually can't get free. The spider may scurry over and bite the insect or wrap it in silk first.)

WITH THE TEACHER

You may wonder why insects and small birds stick to the webs but spiders don't. A spider's body is covered with oil that keeps it from sticking to its own web. Spiders also spin their webs from two kinds of silk. Some threads are sticky, and some are dry. The spider stays on the dry threads!

When spiders leave their webs, they may spin a thin line of silk called a dragline. As a spider travels, its dragline sticks to leaves and branches along the way. Then when it's time to go home, the spider follows the silk trail back to its web.

Why don't spiders get stuck in their own webs?[1] How do spiders travel about and find their way home?[2]

20

COMPREHENDING AS YOU GO

❶ **Understand:** Explaining (A spider's body is covered with oil that keeps it from sticking to its web. A spider also stays on the dry threads instead of the sticky threads.)

❷ **Understand:** Explaining (When a spider travels, it spins a thin line of silk that it sticks to leaves and branches. To go home, it follows the silk back to its web.)

NOTE TAKING 2 • LOCATING INFORMATION

COMPREHENSION PROCESSES

Remember, Understand, Analyze

Locating Information; Identifying—
Topic; Using Headings
Summarizing—Facts

Classifying

PROCEDURES

For each step, demonstrate and guide practice, as needed. Then have students complete the page independently.

Note Taking: Locating Information—Specific Instructions

- Have students read the instructions, then locate the headings and identify the topics in Chapter 2. Have students write the topics in the blanks. Say something like:

Read the instructions. (There are two topics in Chapter 2. Write the topics. Then write three facts about each topic.)

We're going to continue taking research notes. Your notes will help you when you write a great report on spiders. First, let's look in our storybooks and find the headings in Chapter 2. What are the two headings?
(Silk Spinners, Webs at Work)

Yes, these are the two topics that you will take notes on.
You can also use your own words for the topic.
"Silk Spinners" is about the threads that spiders use to make webs.
Instead of the words "Silk Spinners," you could also write "silk thread" for your topic.
What other words could you use as the topic for "Silk Spinners"?

- For each topic, have students write three facts of their choice.
Next, you'll write three facts about each topic. This is what you did for Chapter 1.
It's the fun part because you get to choose the information that you think is interesting.
Look in your book on page 16.

What are some important and interesting facts you could write from the section called "Silk Spinners."
(A spider's web is made from silk. The threads are made in the spinneret . . .)
One fact that I think is amazing is that the tiny threads are stronger than steel thread.
There are a lot of interesting facts we could write about for this first topic.

- Have students save this activity for a report they will write later.

Self-monitoring

Have students check and correct their work.

Spider, Spider, on the Wall

Unit 13 Research Notes
Use with Exercise 2 and Chapter 2

Note Taking 2

Name _____

Locating Information
Icky, Sticky Webs

There are two topics in Chapter 2. Write the topics. Then write three facts about each topic. Look in your storybook on page 16. (You can use the heading or your own words for the topics.)
(Accept any reasonable response.)

Topic: __Spinning Silk__

Fact 1: __silk in spinnerets—liquid__

Fact 2: __silk thread—stronger than steel thread__

Fact 3: __spinnerets at rear of abdomen__

Topic: __Webs at Work__

Fact 1: __build webs to climb from place to place__

Fact 2: __body covered with oil, so doesn't stick__

Fact 3: __spin draglines to follow back home__

Spiders are not insects.
Spiders are classified as
arachnids.

2

PASSAGE READING FLUENCY

FLUENCY

Accuracy, Expression, Rate

PROCEDURES

For each step, demonstrate and guide practice, as needed. Then have students complete the page independently.

Passage Reading—Basic Instructions

- Have students read the practice words.
- Have students finger track and whisper read the story two times—the first time for accuracy and the second time for expression. Have students cross out a spiderweb each time they finish.
- Have students do a one-minute Timed Reading and cross out the timer.

Spider, Spider, on the Wall

Unit 13 Activity 2
Use after Exercise 2 and Chapter 2

Name _____

Passage Reading Fluency

1. Practice these words:

| spinnerets | threads | scurry | fangs |

2. Read the story 2 times. Cross out a spiderweb each time you read the story.

Ming, the Spider, Learns to Use Her Silk

Ming grew up quickly. Soon she was a fine adult spider. She 12
decided that it was fun to be a spider after all. She learned to make 27
silk using her spinnerets. The silk threads she made were stronger than 39
steel threads. She used her silk threads to build a beautiful web. 51

Ming never went hungry. She used her web to trap insects. When 63
an insect flew into her web, she would scurry over and bite the insect 77
with her fangs. She would eat the insect right away or wrap it in silk. 92
By wrapping the insect in silk, Ming could save and eat the insect later. 106

Sometimes, Ming traveled away from her spiderweb. When she 115
did this, she used her silk to make a dragline. When she needed to go 130
home, she just followed the dragline back to her web. Ming always 142
knew how to get home. Ming thought, "I am glad I am a spider." 156

3. Set a timer and see how far you can read in one minute. Then cross out the timer.

6

©2009 Sopris West Educational Services. All Rights Reserved.

ACCURACY PRECEDES RATE
(Reminder)

Students should read the story with a high degree of accuracy before proceeding to Timed Readings. Reading for increased rate before establishing a high degree of accuracy may encourage students to guess at words.

① SOUND REVIEW

Have students read the sounds and key word phrases. Work for accuracy, then fluency.

② ACCURACY AND FLUENCY BUILDING

- For each task, have students say any underlined part, then read the word.
- Set a pace. Then have students read the whole words in each task and column.
- Provide repeated practice, building accuracy first, then fluency.

C1. Rhyming Words

Have students read each set of words and identify what's the same about them.

D1. Word Endings

Have students read any underlined word, then the word with an ending.
Note: Tell students that you drop the e when you add -*ing* to "fascinate."

E1. Tricky Words

- For each Tricky Word, have students use the sounds and word parts they know to silently sound out the word. Use the word in a sentence to help with pronunciation.
- If the word is unfamiliar, tell students the word.

tarantula
Look at the first word. The word is *tarantula*. A large, hairy spider is a . . . *tarantula*.
Read the word three times. (tarantula, tarantula, tarantula)

often	BJ goes to the movies a lot. He goes . . . *often*.
although	Jan had a cast on her broken arm. She went to school . . . *although* . . . it was difficult for her to write.
wander	Mom said, "Don't get lost and . . . *wander* . . . off."

- Have students go back and read the whole words in the column.

③ MULTISYLLABIC WORDS

For each word, have students read the syllables, then the whole word. Use the word in a sentence, as appropriate.

predator	An animal that hunts is a . . . *predator*.
carnivore	An animal that eats meat is a . . . *carnivore*.
rapid	The drummer hit the drum with great speed. His hands were very . . . *rapid*.
bottom	The opposite of top is . . . *bottom*.
tunnel	The moles lived in an underground . . . *tunnel*.
funnel	Mom wanted to pour milk into the bottle, so she used a . . . *funnel*.

④ WORDS IN CONTEXT

For each word, have students use the sounds and word parts they know to silently sound out the word. Then have students read the sentence. Assist, as needed.

⑤ AFFIXES

★Have students practice reading *dis-* and the related words. Use each word in a sentence.

★ = New in this unit

Spider, Spider, On the Wall

Unit 13 Exercise 3
Use before Chapter 3

1. SOUND REVIEW Have students review sounds for accuracy, then for fluency.

A	ea as in bread	au as in astronaut	ph as in phone	ci as in circle	i as in silence
B	ce	gi	oa	kn	oi

2. ACCURACY/FLUENCY BUILDING For each column, have students say any underlined part, then read each word. Next, have them read the column.

A1 New Sound Practice	**B1** Bossy E	**C1** Rhyming Words	**D1** Word Endings	**E1** Tricky Words
b<u>oy</u>	s<u>i</u>zes	icky	<u>cobwebs</u>	tarantula
t<u>oy</u>	h<u>o</u>les	sticky	<u>catching</u>	often
enj<u>oy</u>	sh<u>a</u>pes	tricky	<u>twigs</u>	although
A2 Mixed Practice	sp<u>o</u>kes	r<u>ou</u>nd	<u>rushes</u>	wander
<u>or</u>b	out<u>si</u>de	sound	tangle	**E2** Morphographs & Affixes
cr<u>a</u>b	t<u>a</u>ste	w<u>ou</u>nd	tangled	valu<u>able</u>
w<u>ai</u>ts	t<u>a</u>sty		fascinate	quick<u>ly</u>
fl<u>ow</u>er			fascinating	vibr<u>ation</u>

3. MULTISYLLABIC WORDS Have students read each word part, then read each whole word.

A	pred•a•tor	predator	car•ni•vore	carnivore
B	rap•id	rapid	bot•tom	bottom
C	tun•nel	tunnel	fun•nel	funnel

4. WORDS IN CONTEXT Have students use the sounds and word parts they know to figure out each word. Then have them read each sentence.

A	spi•ral ◎	A <u>spiral</u> is a line that is wound around a center.
B	cer•tain	Are you sure spiders live in attics? Are you <u>certain</u>?
C	prey	The large tarantula spider caught its <u>prey</u> in its web.

5. AFFIXES Have students practice reading "dis-" and the related words.

★dis-	<u>dis</u>cover	<u>dis</u>tance	<u>dis</u>appear	<u>dis</u>aster

APPROPRIATE CORRECTIONS (Reminder)

Write any difficult words on a board or clipboard.

Single-Syllable Pattern Words
Have students identify the difficult sound, then sound out and say the word.

Multisyllabic Words
Draw loops under each word part and then guide practice with your hand.

Tricky Words
Have students sound out or read the word by parts, then say the word. Next have students say, spell, and say the word.

After gently correcting a word with the group, go on to other tasks or words. Return to the difficult word at least three times.

©2009 Sopris West Educational Services. All Rights Reserved.

3

41

COMPREHENSION PROCESSES

Understand, Apply, Evaluate

PROCEDURES

Introducing Vocabulary

⭐ **predator** ⭐ **valuable, vibration** ⭐ **carnivore**

- For each vocabulary word, have students read the word by parts, then read the whole word.
- Read the student-friendly explanations to students as they follow with their fingers. Then have students use the vocabulary word by following the gray text.
- Review and discuss the photos.

"The key to a successful vocabulary program is to use both formal and informal encounters so that attention to vocabulary is happening any time and all the time" (McKeown & Beck, p. 21, 2004).

Content Word Wall

Maintain a content word wall. Start with words from the storybook, then add to the list as students learn additional words related to the theme or topic. Encourage students to use the words in different contexts.

Note: Connections to other content areas will be easy to do because *Read Well* themes and topics are often related to classroom science and social studies instruction.

Students may wish to enhance the word wall by illustrating words with magazine pictures and drawings.

When *Read Well* instruction precedes classroom content-area instruction, the *Read Well* unit provides pre-teaching of vocabulary, inspires interest in a topic, and builds prior knowledge.

If science or social studies instruction follows a related *Read Well* unit, the *Read Well* unit provides review of vocabulary and content knowledge, and may extend content knowledge.

Spiders

predator

protection

senses

⭐ = New in this unit

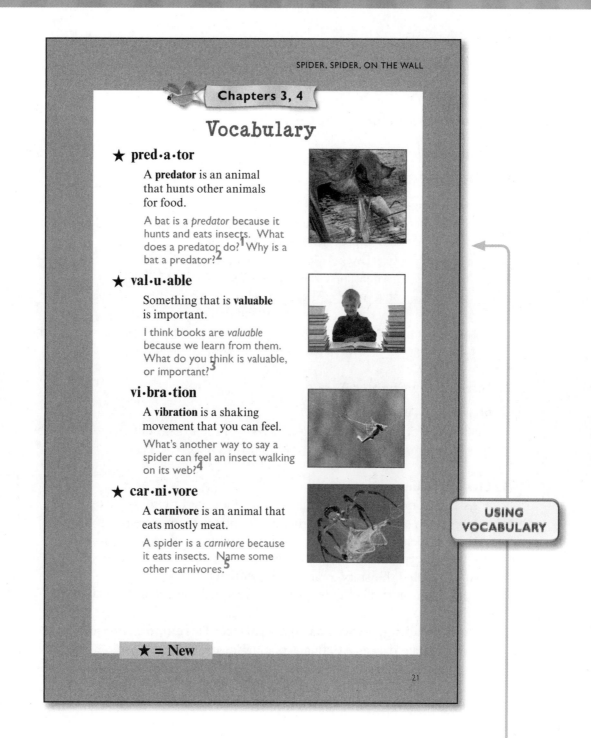

SPIDER, SPIDER, ON THE WALL

Chapters 3, 4

Vocabulary

★ **pred·a·tor**

A **predator** is an animal that hunts other animals for food.

A bat is a *predator* because it hunts and eats insects. What does a predator do?[1] Why is a bat a predator?[2]

★ **val·u·able**

Something that is **valuable** is important.

I think books are *valuable* because we learn from them. What do you think is valuable, or important?[3]

vi·bra·tion

A **vibration** is a shaking movement that you can feel.

What's another way to say a spider can feel an insect walking on its web?[4]

★ **car·ni·vore**

A **carnivore** is an animal that eats mostly meat.

A spider is a *carnivore* because it eats insects. Name some other carnivores.[5]

★ = New

21

USING VOCABULARY

❶ **Understand:** Defining and Using Vocabulary—predator (A predator hunts other animals for food.)

❷ **Understand:** Defining and Using Vocabulary—predator (A bat is a predator because it hunts and eats insects.)

❸ **Evaluate:** Responding; **Apply:** Using Vocabulary—valuable (I think my family is valuable.)

❹ **Apply:** Using Vocabulary—vibration (A spider can feel an insect's vibration on its web.)

❺ **Understand:** Using Vocabulary—carnivore (Lions and sharks are carnivores.)

CHAPTER 3 INSTRUCTIONS
Students read Chapter 3 with the teacher.

COMPREHENSION PROCESSES
Remember, Understand, Apply, Create

PROCEDURES

1. Reviewing Chapter 2

Summarizing—Facts

Review some of the facts learned in Chapter 2. Say something like:

Let's review some of the facts we've learned so far.

How do spiders spin a web? (Spiders push silk out of their spinnerets. When the silk leaves the spider's body, it hardens into a strong thread.

Why do spiders spin webs? (They spin webs to trap food, store food, protect their eggs, climb from place to place, protect themselves, and find their way home.)

What happens to an insect that flies into a spider's web? (An insect that flies into a spiderweb usually can't get free. The spider may scurry over and bite the insect or wrap it up in silk first.)

2. Introducing Chapter 3

Identifying—Title; Inferring

Discuss the title. Say something like: What's the title of this chapter? (Webs, So Strong)
So what are we going to learn more about? (spiderwebs)

3. First Reading
- Ask questions and discuss the story as indicated by the gray text.
- Mix group and individual turns, independent of your voice.
  Have students work toward a group accuracy goal of 0–4 errors.
  Quietly keep track of errors made by all students in the group.
- After reading the story, practice any difficult words.
  Reread the story if students have not reached the accuracy goal.

> **CORRECTING DECODING ERRORS**
> During story reading, gently correct any error, then have students reread the sentence.

4. Second Reading, Short Passage Practice: Developing Prosody
- Demonstrate expressive, fluent reading of the first two paragraphs.
- Guide practice with your voice.
- Provide individual turns while others track with their fingers and whisper read.
- Repeat with one paragraph at a time.

5. Partner or Whisper Reading: Repeated Reading

Before beginning independent work, have students finger track and partner or whisper read.

6. Comprehension and Skill Work

Tell students they will do Research Notes (Note Taking 3) and Comprehension and Skill Activity 3 after they read Chapter 3. Guide practice, as needed. For teacher directions, see pages 49 and 50. Remind students to save their Research Notes for report writing.

7. Homework 3: Repeated Reading

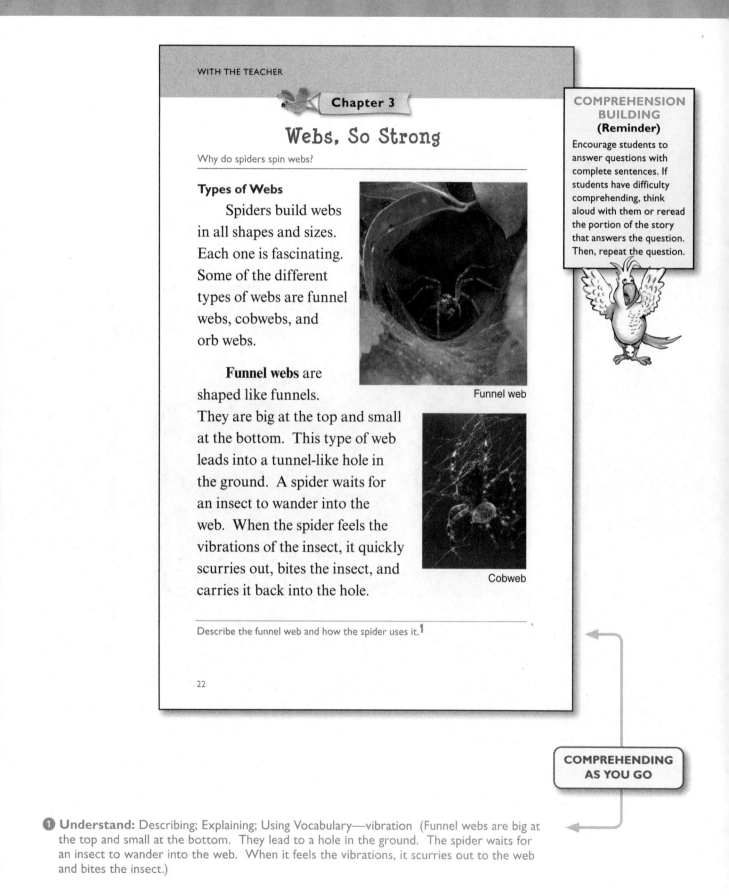

WITH THE TEACHER

Chapter 3

Webs, So Strong

Why do spiders spin webs?

Types of Webs

Spiders build webs in all shapes and sizes. Each one is fascinating. Some of the different types of webs are funnel webs, cobwebs, and orb webs.

Funnel webs are shaped like funnels. They are big at the top and small at the bottom. This type of web leads into a tunnel-like hole in the ground. A spider waits for an insect to wander into the web. When the spider feels the vibrations of the insect, it quickly scurries out, bites the insect, and carries it back into the hole.

Funnel web

Cobweb

Describe the funnel web and how the spider uses it.[1]

22

COMPREHENSION BUILDING (Reminder)
Encourage students to answer questions with complete sentences. If students have difficulty comprehending, think aloud with them or reread the portion of the story that answers the question. Then, repeat the question.

COMPREHENDING AS YOU GO

❶ **Understand:** Describing; Explaining; Using Vocabulary—vibration (Funnel webs are big at the top and small at the bottom. They lead to a hole in the ground. The spider waits for an insect to wander into the web. When it feels the vibrations, it scurries out to the web and bites the insect.)

Cobwebs are tangled webs that have no certain shape. They look like a mess of silk. These are the kind you might see in attics, sheds, and even outside under leaves. Although they look like a mess of silk, they do a good job of catching food for the spider.

Orb webs are the type of web most people think about when they hear spiderweb. An orb web is round and flat. It has a center with spokes going out. It also has many threads of silk wound in a spiral around the center. Spiders can build orb webs in about an hour. They often build new ones every night.

Orb web

Have you ever seen a cobweb?[1] I wonder what kind of spider makes a cobweb. Do you have any questions about cobwebs that the book doesn't answer?[2] Have you ever seen an orb web?[3] Describe an orb web.[4]

23

COMPREHENDING
AS YOU GO

[1] **Remember:** Identifying; **Apply:** Making Connections (Yes, I've seen cobwebs in our storage shed . . .)
[2] **Create:** Generating Ideas, Asking Questions (How do cobwebs catch insects? What kind of spider makes a cobweb?)
[3] **Apply:** Making Connections (Yes, I see orb webs in the trees in the morning . . .)
[4] **Understand:** Describing (An orb web is round and flat, with spokes going out from the center.)

WITH THE TEACHER

Spiders Without Webs

There are some spiders that do not spin webs. With no web to trap food, these spiders have other ways to get food.

Crab spiders can make themselves look like the flower they are resting on. When an insect is near, they quickly catch the insect for a tasty meal.

Crab spider

Tarantulas, the biggest spiders of all, are tricky hunters. Some dig holes in the ground and cover the hole with a trapdoor made of grass or twigs. When an insect or small animal comes near the door, the tarantula rushes out to catch its prey.

Tarantula spider

24

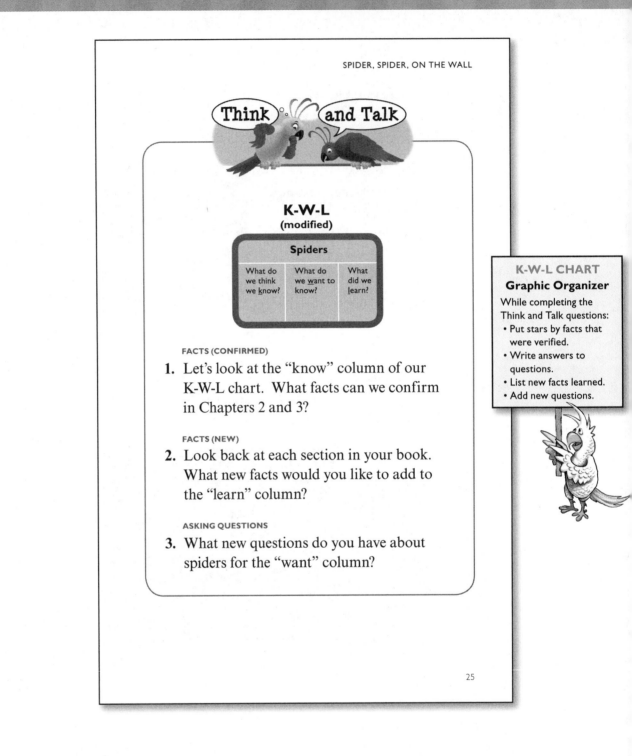

SPIDER, SPIDER, ON THE WALL

Think and **Talk**

K-W-L
(modified)

Spiders		
What do we think we know?	What do we want to know?	What did we learn?

FACTS (CONFIRMED)

1. Let's look at the "know" column of our K-W-L chart. What facts can we confirm in Chapters 2 and 3?

FACTS (NEW)

2. Look back at each section in your book. What new facts would you like to add to the "learn" column?

ASKING QUESTIONS

3. What new questions do you have about spiders for the "want" column?

K-W-L CHART
Graphic Organizer
While completing the Think and Talk questions:
• Put stars by facts that were verified.
• Write answers to questions.
• List new facts learned.
• Add new questions.

25

❶ **Apply:** Locating Information; Verifying—Facts (Spiders have eight legs. Spiders spin webs. Some spiders are small.)

❷ **Understand:** Locating Information; Summarizing—Facts; Using Vocabulary—protect (Spiders make silk with spinnerets. Silk thread is very strong. Spiders build webs for many reasons—to trap food, store food, protect their eggs, climb from place to place, protect themselves, and find their way home. There are three different types of spiderwebs—funnel webs, cobwebs, and orb webs.)

❸ **Create:** Generating Ideas, Asking Questions (How long do spiders live? Can spiders jump?)

NOTE TAKING 3 • COMPARE AND CONTRAST

COMPREHENSION PROCESSES

Remember, Understand, Analyze

Using Graphic Organizer
Comparing/Contrasting

Identifying—Topic; Using Headings
Summarizing—Facts

PROCEDURES

For each step, demonstrate and guide practice, as needed. Then have students complete the page independently.

1. **Compare/Contrast: Matrix—Specific Instructions** (Item 1)
   - Have students read the columns and rows in the matrix.

     A matrix is a chart that organizes information so you can see how something is the same and how it is different. What does a matrix tell? (how something is the same and how it is different)

     This matrix shows how three types of webs are the same and how they are different.

     Put your finger on the first heading and read across. (Type of Web, Shape, Main Use) The matrix will help you compare the types of webs, their shape, and their main use.

     Let's find out the kind of webs we will compare. Go back to the heading that says "Type of Web." Read down the column. (Funnel Web, Cobweb, Orb Web) We're going to find out what is the same and what is different about funnel webs, cobwebs, and orb webs.

     Let's start with the funnel web. Read the information in the box under the heading "Shape." (like a funnel, big at the top, small at the . . .)
     Do you need to look in your book? (no) What should it say? (small at the bottom)
     Now, let's read the information under the heading "Main Use." What's the main use? (to trap food)

     Let's look at the next row. What type of web will you be completing information about? (cobweb) If you don't know the answer, what should you do? (We should look in our books.)

   - Have students fill in the blanks to complete the matrix.
     Remember, when you finish the matrix, what will you be able to tell about the three types of webs? (how they are the same and how they are different)

2. **Note Taking: Locating Information—Basic Instructions** (Item 2)
   - Have students read the directions and look in their books for the heading.
   - Have students select and write three facts from that section of the story.

Spider, Spider, on the Wall

Unit 13 Research Notes

Use with Exercise 3 and Chapter 3

Name _____

Note Taking 3

Compare and Contrast
Webs, So Strong

1. **Complete the following Matrix Chart.** If you need to, look in your storybook.

Type of Web	Shape	Main Use
Funnel Web	• like a funnel • big at the top • small at the _bottom_	to trap food
Cobweb	• no _shape_ • mess of _silk_ • tangled	to trap _food_
Orb Web	• round and _flat_ • a spiral around spokes from center	_to trap food_

(Accept any reasonable response.)

2. **Write three facts about spiders without webs.** Look in your storybook on page 24.

Topic: _Spiders Without Webs_

Fact 1: _Crab spiders make themselves look like flowers to trap food._

Fact 2: _Tarantulas use a trap door to catch prey._

Fact 3: _Not all spiders use webs._

3

PASSAGE READING FLUENCY

FLUENCY

Accuracy, Expression, Rate

PROCEDURES

For each step, demonstrate and guide practice, as needed. Then have students complete the page independently.

Passage Reading—Basic Instructions

- Have students read the practice words.
- Have students finger track and whisper read the story two times—the first time for accuracy and the second time for expression. Have students cross out a spider each time they finish.
- Have students do a one-minute Timed Reading and cross out the timer.

> **ACCURACY PRECEDES RATE (Reminder)**
>
> Students should read the story with a high degree of accuracy before proceeding to Timed Readings. Reading for increased rate before establishing a high degree of accuracy may encourage students to guess at words.

Spider, Spider, on the Wall

Unit 13 Activity 3
Use after Exercise 3 and Chapter 3

Name _____

Passage Reading Fluency

1. Practice these words:

patiently	carnivore	clever	vibrations

2. Read the story 2 times. Cross out a spider each time you read the story.

Fishing Spiders

Floating on a leaf in the pond, a fishing spider patiently waits for   13
its next meal. Like all spiders, the fishing spider is a carnivore. It likes   27
to eat meat. Unlike most spiders, the fishing spider does not spin a web   41
to trap its meal. Instead, this spider has a clever way to catch its food.   56

The fishing spider spends most of its day floating in the water on a   70
leaf. It keeps its front legs touching the water. When the fishing spider   83
feels vibrations, it knows that there is an insect or a tiny fish nearby.   97

If an insect is on the surface of the water, or a tiny fish is swimming   113
close by, the fishing spider quickly grabs it and has a fine meal.   126

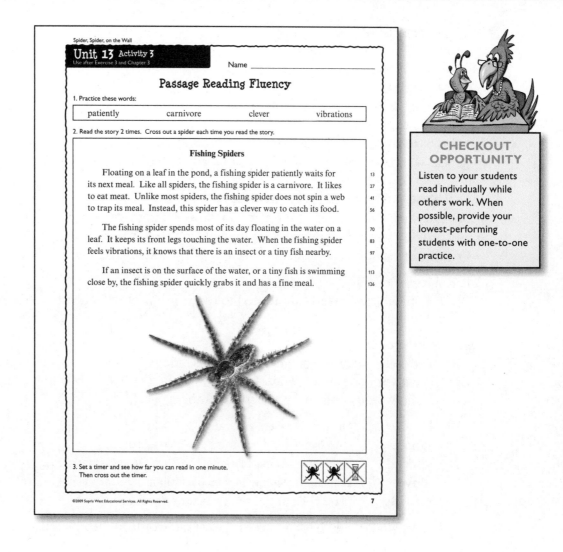

3. Set a timer and see how far you can read in one minute.
Then cross out the timer.

7

CHECKOUT OPPORTUNITY

Listen to your students read individually while others work. When possible, provide your lowest-performing students with one-to-one practice.

❶ SOUND REVIEW

Use selected Sound Cards from Units 1–13.

❷ SOUND PRACTICE

- For each task, have students spell and say the focus sound in the gray bar. For the Bossy <u>E</u>, read the header.
- Next, have students read each underlined sound, the word, then the whole column.
- Repeat with each column, building accuracy first, then fluency.

❸ ACCURACY AND FLUENCY BUILDING

- For each task, have students say any underlined part, then read the word.
- Set a pace. Then have students read the whole words in each task and column.
- Provide repeated practice, building accuracy first, then fluency.

B1. Related Words

Tell students the words are related to the word "protect." Then have them read the words in the set.

E1. Tricky Words

- For each Tricky Word, have students use the sounds and word parts they know to silently sound out the word. Use the word in a sentence to help with pronunciation.
- If the word is unfamiliar, tell students the word.

juice	I like a cold glass of orange . . . *juice.*
whole	I ate every bit. I ate the . . . *whole* . . . thing.
special	Danielle had one stuffed animal that was her favorite. It was . . . *special.*
move	Ben and his family had to pack up and . . . *move.*
moving	Maya and Ana were sad that Ben was . . . *moving.*

- Have students go back and read the whole words in the column.

❹ MULTISYLLABIC WORDS

For each word, have students read the syllables, then the whole word. Use the word in a sentence, as appropriate.

considered	She thought the problem over carefully. She . . . *considered* . . . it.
predator	A tiger is a dangerous . . . *predator.*
Mexico	Many people speak Spanish in . . . *Mexico.*
shelters	The tents were nice, warm . . . *shelters.*

❺ MORPHOGRAPHS AND AFFIXES

- Have students read the underlined part, then the word.
- Repeat practice with whole words, mixing group and individual turns. Build accuracy, then fluency.

❻ GENERALIZATION: READING NEW WORDS IN PARAGRAPHS

- Have students read the paragraph silently, then out loud. Tell students to use the sounds and word parts they know to read any difficult words.
- Repeat practice, as needed.

Spider, Spider, On the Wall

Unit 13 Exercise 4
Use before Chapter 4

1. SOUND REVIEW Use selected Sound Cards from Units 1–13.

2. SOUND PRACTICE In each column, have students spell and say the sound, next say any underlined sound and the word, then read the column.

a as in ago	i as in silence	au	oy	Bossy E
<u>a</u>lone	ti·ny	c<u>au</u>se	b<u>oy</u>	d<u>i</u>ne
<u>a</u>way	Chi·na	bec<u>au</u>se	enj<u>oy</u>	s<u>a</u>fe
<u>a</u>ppears	spi·der	c<u>au</u>ght	destr<u>oy</u>	dragl<u>i</u>ne

3. ACCURACY/FLUENCY BUILDING For each column, have students say any underlined part, then read each word. Next, have them read the column.

A1 Mixed Practice	B1 Related Words	C1 Shifty Words	D1 Word Endings	E1 Tricky Words
h<u>uge</u>	protect	<u>f</u>ang	<u>passes</u>	juice
<u>kn</u>ow	protects	<u>h</u>ang	<u>burn</u>ing	whole
p<u>oi</u>son	protecting	<u>s</u>ang	<u>form</u>s	special
h<u>air</u>s	protection	<u>s</u>ong	<u>toad</u>s	move
s<u>o</u>lid	protected	<u>str</u>ong	live	moving
br<u>ee</u>ze			living	

4. MULTISYLLABIC WORDS Have students read each word part, then read each whole word.

Ⓐ con·si·dered	considered	pred·a·tor	predator
Ⓑ Mex·i·co	Mexico	shel·ters	shelters

5. MORPHOGRAPHS AND AFFIXES Have students read each underlined part, then the word.

Ⓐ -ous	fam<u>ous</u>	nerv<u>ous</u>	danger<u>ous</u>	curi<u>ous</u>
Ⓑ easi<u>ly</u>	valu<u>able</u>	<u>re</u>hooked	certain<u>ly</u>	amazing<u>ly</u>

> **TEACHER: SELF-MONITORING (Reminder)**
> - Are you gently correcting all errors?
> - Are you returning to difficult words for three correct responses?
> - Are you mixing group and individual turns?
> - Are you repeating practice until students are accurate and fluent?
> - Are you preteaching the lowest performers in your group?
>
> (See *Getting Started* to understand why these strategies are critical to student success.)

6. GENERALIZATION Have students read the paragraph silently, then out loud. (New words: mouse, trapped, itch)

Mark the mouse was trapped and in danger! He was stuck in the sticky web of a tarantula. Mark started to itch, but he stayed still. He didn't want the gigantic spider to notice him. Just then, the tarantula looked at him. "Oh, no," thought Mark. "I'm going to be eaten!"

Suddenly, a lizard darted by. As the tarantula turned toward the lizard, Mark pulled against the sticky web with all his might. He felt the threads break, and he was free!

CHAPTER 4 INSTRUCTIONS
Students read Chapter 4 with the teacher.

COMPREHENSION PROCESSES
Remember, Understand, Apply, Analyze, Create

PROCEDURES

1. Reviewing Chapter 3

Summarizing—Facts
Review some of the facts learned in Chapter 3. Say something like:
Name some types of webs. (funnel webs, cobwebs, orb webs)
Do all spiders spin webs? (no)

2. Introducing Chapter 4

Identifying—Title; Inferring—Topic
- Read and discuss the title. Say something like:
  What's the title of this chapter? (A Spider's Life)
  What do you think this chapter will be about?
- Discuss the gray text questions under the chapter title.

3. First Reading
- Ask questions and discuss the story as indicated by the gray text.
- Mix group and individual turns, independent of your voice.
  Have students work toward a group accuracy goal of 0–6 errors.
  Quietly keep track of errors made by all students in the group.
- After reading the story, practice any difficult words.
  Reread the story if students have not reached the accuracy goal.

4. Second Reading, Timed Readings: Repeated Reading

- As time allows, have students do Timed Readings while others follow along.
- Time individuals for 30 seconds and encourage each child to work for a personal best.
- Count the number of words read correctly in 30 seconds (words read minus errors).
  Multiply by two to determine words correct per minute. Record student scores.

5. Partner or Whisper Reading: Repeated Reading

Before beginning independent work, have students finger track and partner or whisper read.

6. Comprehension and Skill Work
Tell students they will do Research Notes (Note Taking 4) and Comprehension and Skill Activity 4 after they read Chapter 4. Guide practice, as needed. For teacher directions, see pages 61 and 62. Remind students to save their Research Note pages for report writing.

7. Homework 4: Repeated Reading

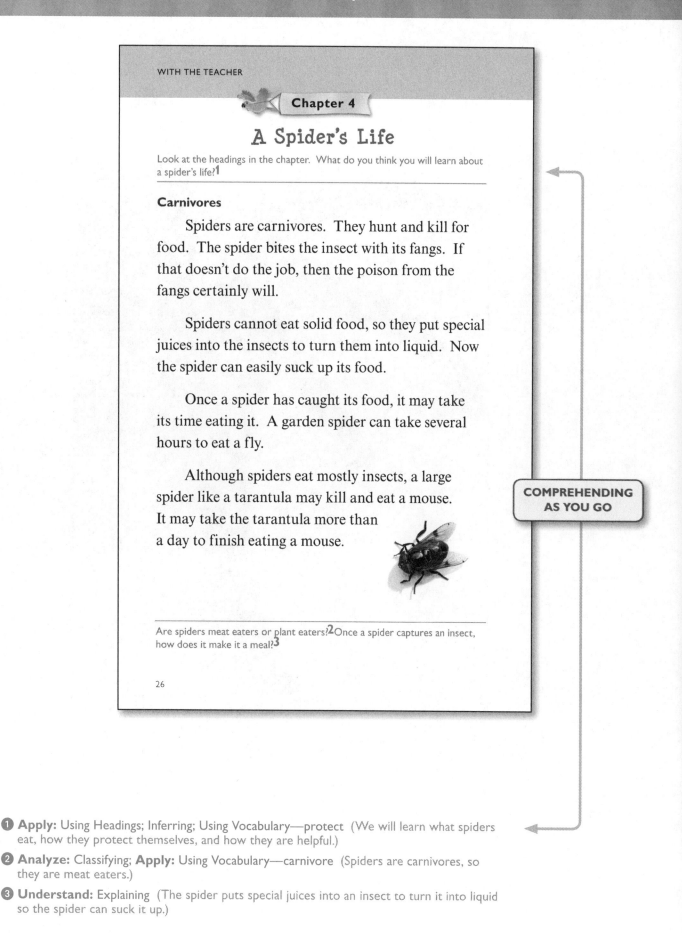

Chapter 4

A Spider's Life

Look at the headings in the chapter. What do you think you will learn about a spider's life?[1]

Carnivores

Spiders are carnivores. They hunt and kill for food. The spider bites the insect with its fangs. If that doesn't do the job, then the poison from the fangs certainly will.

Spiders cannot eat solid food, so they put special juices into the insects to turn them into liquid. Now the spider can easily suck up its food.

Once a spider has caught its food, it may take its time eating it. A garden spider can take several hours to eat a fly.

Although spiders eat mostly insects, a large spider like a tarantula may kill and eat a mouse. It may take the tarantula more than a day to finish eating a mouse.

Are spiders meat eaters or plant eaters?[2] Once a spider captures an insect, how does it make it a meal?[3]

26

COMPREHENDING AS YOU GO

❶ **Apply:** Using Headings; Inferring; Using Vocabulary—protect (We will learn what spiders eat, how they protect themselves, and how they are helpful.)

❷ **Analyze:** Classifying; **Apply:** Using Vocabulary—carnivore (Spiders are carnivores, so they are meat eaters.)

❸ **Understand:** Explaining (The spider puts special juices into an insect to turn it into liquid so the spider can suck it up.)

SPIDER, SPIDER, ON THE WALL

27

WITH THE TEACHER

Protection

Do spiders have to worry about getting eaten themselves? They certainly do. Frogs, toads, lizards, and some birds eat spiders. Sometimes spiders eat other spiders!

Spiders have many ways to get away from animals that are trying to eat them. If a predator appears, spiders can drop down on their draglines. They hang by the line until the danger passes. Spiders live alone, so they must protect themselves.

Some tarantulas have tiny hooked hairs on their legs. They rub these on a predator's face and body to cause a burning itch.

How do spiders *protect* themselves from *predators?* **1**

28

COMPREHENDING
AS YOU GO

1 Understand: Explaining; Using Vocabulary—protect, predator (Spiders protect themselves in several ways. They can drop down on their draglines to get away from danger. Some have hooked hairs that make predators itch.)

SPIDER, SPIDER, ON THE WALL

Sometimes a predator breaks off a spider's leg. That's no problem for the spider. It can live with seven legs. Sometimes when a leg is hurt, the spider uses its other legs to break off the bad one.

Helpful Spiders

Spiders are a huge help to people and other living things on Earth. They protect whole crops of foods by eating insects that can destroy the crops.

In China, the farmers know that they need spiders to protect their crops from insects. The spiders are considered so valuable that some farmers build shelters to help the spiders get through the cold winter. In Mexico, some people keep the webs of spiders near their homes to protect them from flies and other insects.

Spiders are helpful. Protecting these special creatures protects other forms of life.

Have you ever seen a seven-legged spider?[1] What do you think happened to it?[2] What are some reasons people think spiders are valuable?[3]

29

COMPREHENDING AS YOU GO

1 **Apply:** Making Connections (Yes, I have. No, I haven't.)

2 **Apply:** Inferring, Explaining (It probably hurt its leg and broke it off.)

3 **Understand:** Explaining; Using Vocabulary—valuable, destroy (People value spiders because they eat insects that can destroy crops.)

WITH THE TEACHER

Spider, Spider, all alone,
Building a web for your home.
Webs so sticky and so fine,
Insects trapped on which to dine.
Farmers' crops grow tall and sweet,
Safe from the insects that you eat.

Spider, Spider, in the trees,
Spinning a web in the breeze.
Hundreds and hundreds of feet long,
Amazingly thin, yet so strong.
When it is food that you need,
Your web will help, indeed!

30

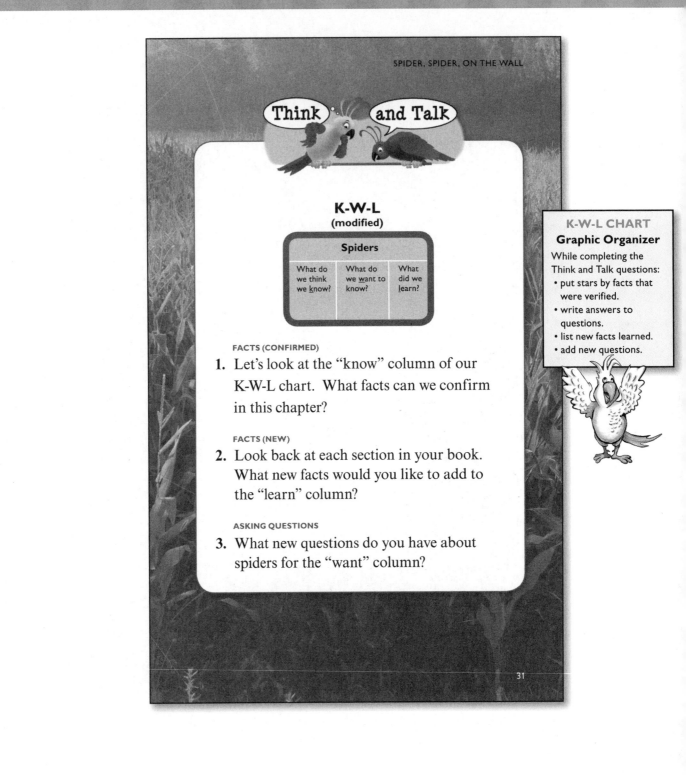

SPIDER, SPIDER, ON THE WALL

Think and **Talk**

K-W-L
(modified)

Spiders		
What do we think we <u>know</u>?	What do we <u>want</u> to know?	What did we <u>learn</u>?

FACTS (CONFIRMED)

1. Let's look at the "know" column of our K-W-L chart. What facts can we confirm in this chapter?

FACTS (NEW)

2. Look back at each section in your book. What new facts would you like to add to the "learn" column?

ASKING QUESTIONS

3. What new questions do you have about spiders for the "want" column?

K-W-L CHART
Graphic Organizer
While completing the Think and Talk questions:
• put stars by facts that were verified.
• write answers to questions.
• list new facts learned.
• add new questions.

31

❶ **Apply:** Locating Information; Verifying—Facts (Spiders are helpful. They eat insects that can destroy food crops.)

❷ **Understand:** Locating Information; Summarizing—Facts; Using Vocabulary—carnivore, protect, predator (Spiders are carnivores, but they also have to protect themselves from other predators. Spiders put special juices into their food to turn it to liquid. Spiders can live with only seven legs.)

❸ **Create:** Generating Ideas, Asking Questions (Why can't a spider eat solid food? What kinds of spiders are poisonous to humans?)

NOTE TAKING 4 • LOCATING INFORMATION

COMPREHENSION PROCESSES

Remember, Understand

Identifying—Topic; Using Headings
Summarizing—Facts

Spider, Spider, on the Wall
Unit 13 Research Notes   Use with Exercise 4 and Chapter 4

Note Taking 4

Name _____

Locating Information
A Spider's Life

The three topics in Chapter 4 are: Carnivores, Protection, and Helpful Spiders. Select two topics. Then write three facts about each topic.
(Accept any reasonable response.)

Topic: _Carnivores_____

Fact 1: _use poison from fangs to kill their prey_____

Fact 2: _change solid food to liquid and suck up food___

Fact 3: _mostly eat insects_____

Topic: _Helpful Spiders_____

Fact 1: _help protect crops by eating insects_____

Fact 2: _sheltered by people in China_____

Fact 3: _Some people in Mexico keep webs near their homes._

4   ©2009 Sopris West Educational Services. All Rights Reserved.

PROCEDURES

For each step, demonstrate and guide practice, as needed. Then have students complete the page independently.

Note Taking: Locating Information—Specific Instructions

• Have students read the instructions, select two topics, and take notes.

Everyone, read the directions. (The three topics in Chapter 4 are: Carnivores, Protection, and Helpful Spiders. Select two topics. Then write three facts about each topic.)

You already know how to do this. Remember, your notes will help you write a really interesting report on spiders, so be sure to write down facts that you think are interesting and important.

• Have students save this activity for a report they will write later.

Self-monitoring

Have students check and correct their work.

MAIN IDEA AND SUPPORTING DETAILS

COMPREHENSION PROCESSES
Remember, Understand, Apply

WRITING TRAITS
Conventions—Complete Sentence, Capital, Period

PROCEDURES
For each step, demonstrate and guide practice, as needed. Then have students complete the page independently.

1. **Topic: Answering Questions—Basic Instructions** (Item 1)
   - Have students read the paragraph.
   - Have students read the question and write the topic in the blank.

2. **Main Idea/Supporting Details: Hierarchy Chart—Basic Instructions** (Item 2)
   - Have students fill in the blanks to complete the supporting details. Remind students that they do not need to write in complete sentences when they list the supporting details.
   - Have students select and complete the main idea. Have them select the answer that best tells where spiders live. Say something like:
   Before you complete the main idea sentence, review all the supporting details you've written. Next, find the answer that tells the most important thing about where spiders live. Then write the main idea.

3. **Main Idea: Sentence Writing—Specific Instructions** (Item 3)
   Have students write the main idea. Remind them to start with a capital and end with a period.

Spider, Spider, on the Wall

Unit 13 Activity 4
Use after Exercise 4 and Chapter 4

Name _____

Main Idea and Supporting Details

> Spiders can be found in many different places all over the world. Some spiders live in gardens. Others live in deserts. Still others live in the mountains. Many live in your homes. Spiders can live in many places, but they usually live alone.

Identifying—Topic

(Accept any reasonable response.)
1 What is this paragraph about? where spiders live

(Accept any reasonable response.)
2 Supporting Details: Spiders live in . . .
List the details.

Using Graphic Organizer Identifying— Supporting Details Inferring—Main Idea; Sentence Completion Sentence Writing

- gardens

- deserts

- mountains

- our homes

Main Idea:

Spiders live . . .

all over the world.
_____

○ in deserts.
● all over the world.
○ in gardens.

3 Write the main idea. Be sure to start your sentence with a capital letter.

Spiders live all over the world.
_____

8

CHECKOUT OPPORTUNITY

Listen to your students read individually while others work. When possible, provide your lowest-performing students with one-to-one practice.

❶ SOUND REVIEW

❷ SHIFTY WORD BLENDING

For each word, have students say the underlined sound. Then have them sound out the word smoothly and say it. Use the words in sentences, as appropriate.

❸ ACCURACY AND FLUENCY BUILDING

- For each task, have students say any underlined part, then read the word.
- Set a pace. Then have students read the whole words in each task and column.
- Provide repeated practice, building accuracy first, then fluency.

C1, D1. Word Endings

- For column C1, have students read each underlined word, then the word with an ending. Use the word in a sentence, as needed.
- For the column D1, have students read each word set. *Note:* Tell students to note the spelling changes when endings are added to these words.

E1. Tricky Words

- For each Tricky Word, have students use the sounds and word parts they know to silently sound out the word. Use the word in a sentence to help with pronunciation.
- If the word is unfamiliar, tell students the word.

washed

Look at the first word. This word is tricky, but I think you can get it. Thumbs up when you know the word. Angel's pants were dirty, so she . . . *washed* . . . them.
Say it three times. (washed, washed, washed)

rhymes

Look at the next word. The word is *rhymes*.
"Humpty Dumpty" and "Jack and Jill" are both nursery . . . *rhymes*.
Say it three times. (rhymes, rhymes, rhymes)

worse	The opposite of better is . . . *worse*.
caught	We went fishing, and Dad . . . *caught* . . . three fish.
enough	Are you still hungry? Did you get . . . *enough* . . . to eat?

- Have students go back and read the whole words in the column.

❹ WORDS IN CONTEXT

For each word, have students use the sounds and word parts they know to silently sound out the word. Then have students read the sentence. Assist, as needed.

❺ MORPHOGRAPHS AND AFFIXES

- Have students read the underlined part, then the word.
- For the words "thoughtful" and "biweekly," review the meaning of the morphographs. Say something like:
  What does -*ful* mean? (full of) Thoughtful means full of . . . thought.
  What does *bi*- mean? (two) So biweekly means two times a . . . week.
- Repeat practice with whole words, mixing group and individual turns. Build accuracy, then fluency.

Spider, Spider, On the Wall

Unit 13 Exercise 5a
Use before Exercise 5b

1. SOUND REVIEW Have students review sounds for accuracy, then for fluency.

A	ow as in snow	ge as in page	-y as in baby	aw as in paw	o as in open
B	ew	u_e	-dge	igh	ir

2. SHIFTY WORD BLENDING For each word, have students say the underlined part, sound out smoothly, then read the word.

jerk	perk	peak	peal	pail

3. ACCURACY/FLUENCY BUILDING For each column, have students say any underlined part, then read each word. Next, have them read the column.

A1 Mixed Practice	B1 Rhyming Words	C1 Word Endings	D1 Word Endings	E1 Tricky Words
boy	itsy	catching	dry	washed
crown	bitsy	insects	dried	rhymes
fifth		messed		worse
broke	etch	completed	weave	caught
yellow	fetch	startled	weaving	enough
yum	sketch			
			tumble	
			tumbling	

4. WORDS IN CONTEXT Have students use the sounds and word parts they know to figure out each word. Then have them read each sentence.

A	pour	Will you please pour me a cup of tea?
B	down·pour	A lot of rain that falls in a short time is called a downpour.
C	wa·ter·spout	A pipe for carrying water from a roof is called a waterspout.

5. MORPHOGRAPHS AND AFFIXES Have students read the underlined word part, then the word.

A	began	lovely	thoughtful	famous	display
B	exactly	biweekly	decide	rework	vibration

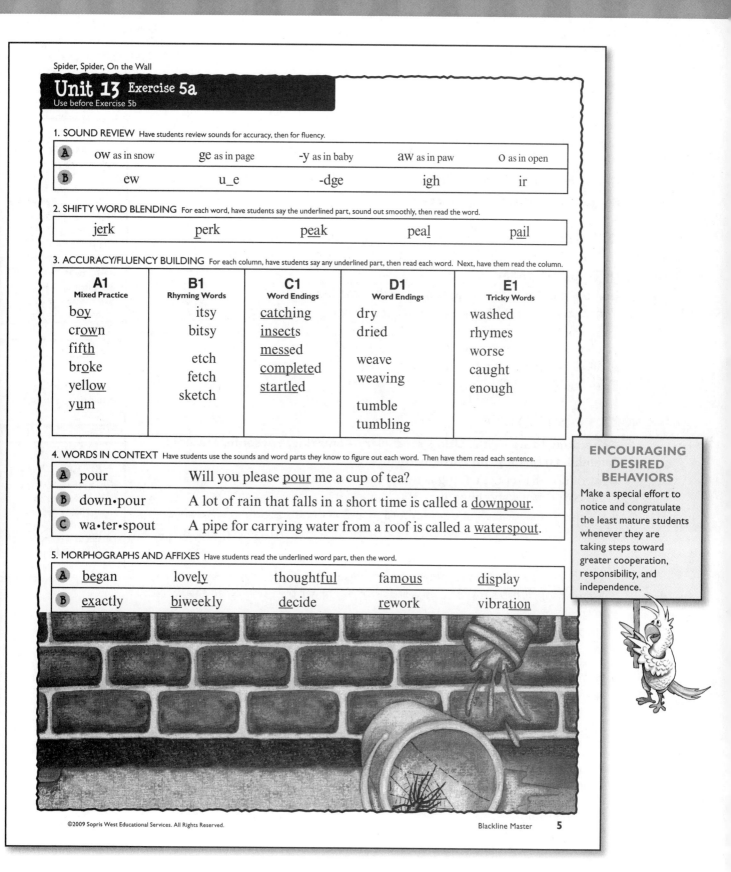

Blackline Master **5**

> **ENCOURAGING DESIRED BEHAVIORS**
>
> Make a special effort to notice and congratulate the least mature students whenever they are taking steps toward greater cooperation, responsibility, and independence.

REPORT WRITING

PURPOSE

This lesson provides explicit instruction in how to select a title and write the introductory paragraph of a report. The lesson prepares students for Comprehension and Skill Work.

COMPREHENSION PROCESSES

Remember, Understand, Create

PROCEDURES

1 INTRODUCTION

Introduce the report-writing activity. Say something like:

Today, you are going to use your notes to start writing a report on spiders.
Like a Fact Summary, a report is a great way to remember and understand factual information. Once you've written about a subject, you've started to become an expert on it. Today, we're going to start writing a report together.
Then you'll have time to start your own report.

2 COVER AND TITLE

Generating Ideas—Title; Using Vocabulary—amazing, awesome, arachnid, splendid, fascinating, predator, carnivore

• Introduce the report-writing activity. Guide writing the title. Show students the cover. Say something like:

It's always fun to think of titles for a report. Sometimes authors like to write the title of their report after they've written it. Other writers like to title their reports first.

We've learned a lot about spiders, so let's figure out a title first. Look at the Word Bank. It has some snazzy words that we might try using. Read the words in the Word Bank.

(amazing, arachnid, splendid, fascinating, predator, carnivore)
We might call our report "Amazing Arachnids."

• Have students brainstorm other titles in partners or as a group.
• Select a title and write it on the group report.

Remember to keep all your great ideas in mind when you write your own report. I'm going to use "Cool Carnivores" as my title. It doesn't have the word *spider* in it, but the picture helps tell the reader what this report is about.

Write "Cool Carnivores" for the title.

• Write the authors' names on the report.

PREP NOTES

To demonstrate how to write a report, use an overhead of page 6 in student *Exercise Book 3*, write on a transparency placed over the page, or use a paper copy.

RESEARCH NOTES

Students will need their research notes to complete this Focus Lesson.

LESSON SEQUENCING

If your schedule allows, you may wish to do today's Story Reading and then do the Focus Lesson so it immediately precedes students' own work on their reports.

Fluency

Unit 13 Exercise 5b (Focus Lesson)
Use after Exercise 5a and before Comprehension and Skill Work: Report Writing

FOCUS LESSON
Skills and Strategies

Title Page

Title Page: Write the title of your report and your name on the lines below.

Cool Carnivores

by _____ Ms. Smith's Group _____

STOP
Don't write in your Exercise Book.

Word Bank

amazing
arachnid
splendid
fascinating
predator
carnivore

Date _____ 11-08-10 _____

REPORT WRITING (*continued*)

❸ INTRODUCTION

Identifying—Topic, Facts; Locating Information; Using Vocabulary—habit

- Have students read and complete the introductory sentence.

  Read the first direction for the Introduction. (1. Introduce the subject . . .)

  First, we're going to introduce our subject. Everyone, what's our subject? (spiders)

  Now, read the first sentence. (Spiders are *blank* creatures.)

  Think of a snazzy word that we can use in the blank. (splendid, fascinating . . .)

  Those are all great snazzy words. Keep them in mind when you write your own report. I think I'll use the word *fascinating*. **Write "fascinating" in the blank.**

  Next, we need to write at least one fascinating fact to interest our readers.

  The purpose of our introduction is to get the reader hooked.

  Look through your notes and find a fact that was really cool.

  When you find a fact you thought was incredibly interesting, put your thumbs up.

  What are some of the facts you came up with? (Spiders have poisonous fangs. Their legs come out of their heads . . .) Those are all cool facts. I think I'll write, "They make silk thread that is stronger than steel."

  Write "They make silk thread that is stronger than steel."

  Demonstrate and guide how to elaborate.

  I have a lot of space left. I think I'll write another fact.

  I don't want to confuse our readers, so I think I'll write more about the spider's silk thread. Does anyone remember another interesting fact about a spider's thread?

  (Spiders make a lot of it.)

  Yes, that's right. Does anyone remember how much?

  Where could we look to find the answer? (in our notes, in our storybooks)

  Who can find that fact—how much thread does a spider make?

  When you find the information, thumbs up.

  [Jackie], what did you find out? (A spider makes hundreds of feet of thread.)

  That's great. I'm going to add that fact: Spiders make hundreds of feet of thread.

  Write "They also make hundreds of feet of thread."

- Have students select two topics from their notes to write about.

  We have one more direction to follow to complete our introduction.

  Everyone, go to the top of the page and read the next direction.

  (2. Next, select and introduce two topics.)

- Have students brainstorm topics to write about.

  You are going to look at your research notes and choose two topics that you want to write about. Selecting topics is very important. Look through your notes and pick two topics that you think have especially interesting facts.

  I've chosen the topics of webs and carnivores for us to write about. So to introduce our topic, we could write, "This report is about spider webs and carnivores." That's a little boring. Can you help me figure out a few sentences that are more interesting?

  Write "This report is about the icky sticky webs that spiders spin. It is also about their strange eating habits."

- Have students read the introductory paragraph. Remind them that they will get to use all their good ideas in their own reports during independent work.

Fluency

Unit 13 Exercise 5c (Focus Lesson)
Use after Exercise 5b

FOCUS
LESSON
Skills and
Strategies

Introduction

STOP

Don't write
in your
Exercise
Book.

◆ **INTRODUCTION** • 1. Introduce the subject. Include at least one fascinating
fact to interest the reader.
2. Next, select and introduce two topics.

Spiders are __fascinating__ creatures. They
make silk thread that is stronger than steel. They
also make hundreds of feet of thread.

This report is about __the icky sticky webs that
spiders spin. It is also about their strange eating
habits.__

Blackline Master **7**

FLUENCY PASSAGE INSTRUCTIONS

This Story Reading targets fluency. Students do repeated readings to improve accuracy, expression, and rate.

COMPREHENSION PROCESSES

Apply

PROCEDURES

1. Introduction

Making Connections, Predicting

Ask students whether they've heard the nursery rhymes "The Itsy Bitsy Spider" and "Jack and Jill." Say something like:

Today's reading begins with two nursery rhymes that you've probably heard.

How many of you know "The Itsy Bitsy Spider"?

What happened to the spider? (It got washed down the waterspout . . .)

How many of you know "Jack and Jill"? What happened to Jack and Jill? (They fell . . .)

After you read the rhymes, you'll read a fun story about the itsy bitsy spider and Jack and Jill. What do you think will happen when the spider ends up in Jack and Jill's pail?

> **PARTNER READING— CHECKOUT OPPORTUNITY**
>
> While students are Partner Reading, listen to individuals read the passage. Work on accuracy and fluency, as needed.

2. Warm-Up: Partner Reading or Whisper Reading

Have students finger track and partner or whisper read the nursery rhymes on page 33 ("The Itsy Bitsy Spider," "Jack and Jill") and the fluency passage, "Down the Spout Again."

3. First Reading

- Ask questions as indicated by the gray text.
- Mix group and individual turns, independent of your voice.
  Have students work toward a group accuracy goal of 0–2 errors.
- After reading the story, practice any difficult words.
  Reread the story if students have not reached the accuracy goal.

4. Second Reading, Short Passage Practice: Developing Prosody

- Demonstrate reading the first paragraph with expression and fluency.
- Have students choral read the first paragraph. Encourage reading with expression and fluency.
- Repeat with second paragraph.

5. Third Reading, Group Timed Readings: Repeated Reading

- Select a page. Have students whisper read for a one-minute Timed Reading. Tell students to go back to the top of the page and keep reading until the minute is up.
- Have students put their finger on the last word they read and count the number of words read correctly in one minute.
- Have students try to beat their score with a second Timed Reading of the same page.

6. Comprehension and Skill

Tell students they will do Report Writing (Title Page and Introduction) after they read "Down the Spout Again." (For teacher directions, see page 76.)

7. Homework 5: Repeated Reading

The Itsy Bitsy Spider

The itsy bitsy spider
Went up the waterspout.
Down came the rain
And washed the spider out.
Out came the sun
And dried up all the rain.
And the itsy bitsy spider
Went up the spout again.

Jack and Jill

Jack and Jill went up the hill
To fetch a pail of water.
Jack fell down and broke
his crown,
And Jill came tumbling after.

33

WITH THE TEACHER

Fluency

Down the Spout Again

by Itsty Bitsy (aka Karen Akiyama-Paik)
illustrated by Karen Perrins

"Here I go," said the itsy bitsy spider. "Up 　9
the waterspout again." At the top, Itsy Bitsy 　17
began to spin a web for the fifth time. It was a 　29
lot of work, but the waterspout was the perfect 　38
spot for catching insects. 　42

As the spider completed her web, she felt 　50
vibrations. She had caught her lunch! "Yum," 　57
said the spider as she started to spin silk around 　67
the fly. 　69

Suddenly, a downpour washed the spider 　75
down the spout again. This time, Itsy Bitsy 　83
landed at the bottom of a yellow pail. 　91

Out came the sun and dried up all the rain, 　101
but this time the itsy bitsy spider said, "Enough 　110
is enough. No more waterspouts. This time, I 　118
will spin my web in the yellow pail!" 　126

34

DOWN THE SPOUT AGAIN

35

Fluency

Itsy Bitsy got to work again, weaving a lovely 9
web. A sudden jerk startled her and messed up 18
her web. 20

A boy named Jack had picked up the pail. 29
Jack and his sister Jill were going up the hill to 40
fetch a pail of water. 45

"Now what?" thought Itsy Bitsy. Jack 51
was swinging the pail and making her feel sick. 60
Then things went from bad to worse. Jack 68
fell down and so did Jill. Then the pail went 78
tumbling after! 80

You know what happened to Jack and Jill. Can you guess what happened to the spider?[1]

36

COMPREHENDING AS YOU GO

1 **Apply:** Inferring (The spider fell down the hill too . . .)

DOWN THE SPOUT AGAIN

37

TITLE PAGE

COMPREHENSION PROCESSES

Remember, Understand, Apply, Create

WRITING TRAITS

**Ideas and Content
Organization—Topic,
Supporting Details
Word Choice
Conventions—Complete Sentence,
Capital, Period
Presentation**

> ### SPECIAL NOTE
> Students will now use their notes to write a report. Pull out their Report Writing pages to create report folders.

Generating Ideas—Title

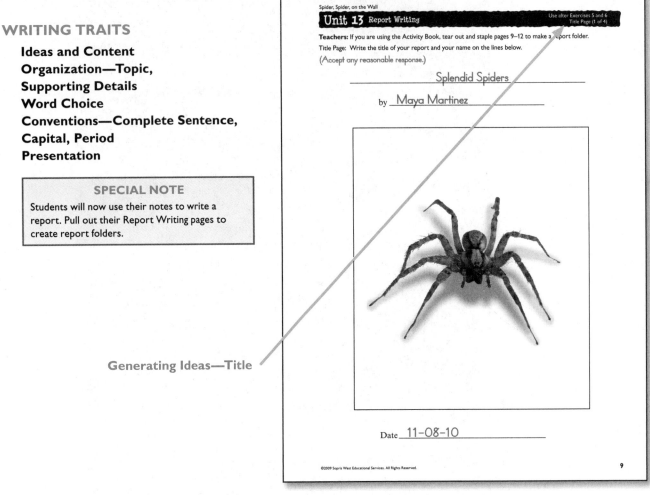

Spider, Spider, on the Wall

Unit 13 Report Writing

Use after Exercises 5 and 6
Title Page (1 of 4)

Teachers: If you are using the Activity Book, tear out and staple pages 9–12 to make a report folder.

Title Page: Write the title of your report and your name on the lines below.
(Accept any reasonable response.)

Splendid Spiders

by Maya Martinez

Date 11–08–10

©2009 Sopris West Educational Services. All Rights Reserved.

9

PROCEDURES

For each step, demonstrate and guide practice, if needed. Then have students complete the page independently.

Note: Students will use their Unit 13 Research Notes (Note Taking 1–4) to complete this activity.

1. **Report Writing: Title Page—Specific Instructions**
   - Have students find their Unit 13 Research Notes (Note Taking 1–4) to complete this activity.
   - Remind students they are going to complete the cover and the introductory paragraph of their report. (See Exercise 5b.)
   - Have students write their names, the date, and the title if they know what they want to call their report. (Some students may choose to write their title after they've written their report.) Tell students to use their best handwriting.

INTRODUCTION

**Generating Ideas—Introduction
Identifying—Subject/Topic; Explaining
Sentence Completion
Sentence Writing; Paragraph Writing**

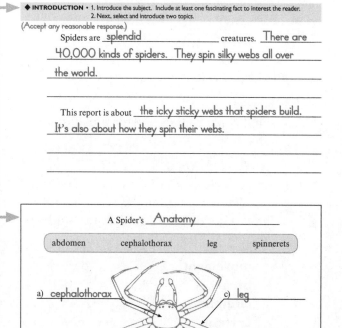

Spider, Spider, on the Wall

Unit 13 Report Writing

Introduction (2 of 4)

◆ **INTRODUCTION** • 1. Introduce the subject. Include at least one fascinating fact to interest the reader.
2. Next, select and introduce two topics.

(Accept any reasonable response.)

Spiders are ___splendid___ creatures. There are 40,000 kinds of spiders. They spin silky webs all over the world.

This report is about ___the icky sticky webs that spiders build.___ It's also about how they spin their webs.

**Using Graphic Organizer
Identifying—Topic; Explaining
Using Vocabulary—cephalothorax**

A Spider's ___Anatomy___

| abdomen | cephalothorax | leg | spinnerets |

a) cephalothorax
b) abdomen
c) leg
d) spinnerets

10

©2009 Sopris West Educational Services. All Rights Reserved.

2. **Report Writing: Introduction—Specific Instructions**
   - Have students review the directions for writing the introduction. Remind students to start sentences with a capital and end with a period.
   - Have students write the first paragraph of the introduction by completing the first sentence and writing one or two interesting facts about spiders.
   - Have students review their notes and select two interesting topics to write about.

3. **Diagram: Labeling—Specific Instructions**
   - Tell students to read the words in the gray shaded box, then fill in the blank to complete the diagram's title.
   - Have students label the parts of the spider using the words in the box.
     Put your finger on the diagram of the spider.
     You are going to label the parts of a spider for your report.
     What's a snazzy word for body parts? (anatomy)
     So for your title, you can write, A Spider's . . . (Anatomy).
     Now read the words in the box. (abdomen, cephalothorax . . .)
     Those are hard words to spell! How will you know how to spell them?
     (Copy them carefully from the box.)

MARKING TOPICS

You may wish to have students mark the topics they choose in their research notes with:
- sticky notes
- happy faces
- highlighters

① SOUND REVIEW

Have students read the sounds and key word phrases. Work for accuracy, then fluency.

② SHIFTY WORD BLENDING

For each word, have students say the underlined sound. Then have them sound out the word smoothly and say it. Use the words in sentences, as appropriate.

③ ACCURACY AND FLUENCY BUILDING

- For each task, have students say any underlined part, then read the word.
- Set a pace. Then have students read the whole words in each task and column.
- Provide repeated practice, building accuracy first, then fluency.

C1. Related Words

Tell students these words are all related to the word "protect." Have students read the word set.

D1, E1. Tricky Words

- For each Tricky Word, have students use the sounds and word parts they know to silently sound out the word. Use the word in a sentence to help with pronunciation.
- If the word is unfamiliar, tell students the word.

special	Everyone likes to feel . . . *special.*
movement	An insect got in the spider's web, and the spider felt its . . . *movement.*
break	When I'm tired, I take a . . . *break.*
climbed	The little kitten . . . *climbed* . . . up the tree.
certain	Are you sure? Are you . . . *certain?*
although	Harry was still hungry . . . *although* . . . he just ate.
group	Tonya's brother belongs to a volunteer . . . *group.*
toward	The opposite of *away from* is . . . *toward.*
actually	There were fewer than ten kids on the playground. There were . . . *actually* . . . four.
usually	What you do most of the time is what you . . . *usually* . . . do.

- Have students go back and read the whole words in the column.

④ WORD ENDINGS

Have students read the underlined word, then the word with an ending. Use each word in a sentence, as needed.

⑤ MORPHOGRAPHS AND AFFIXES

- Have students read the underlined part, then the word.
- Repeat practice with whole words, mixing group and individual turns. Build accuracy, then fluency.

Centipede and Grandmother Spider

Unit 13 Exercise 6a
Use before Exercise 6b

1. SOUND REVIEW Have students review sounds for accuracy, then for fluency.

Ⓐ	ea as in bread	ew as in crew	ph as in phone	o as in open	i as in silence
Ⓑ	gi	-dge	kn	ue	u_e

2. SHIFTY WORD BLENDING For each word, have students say the underlined part, sound out smoothly, then read the word.

<u>ea</u>rs	<u>h</u>ears	h<u>ai</u>rs	<u>p</u>airs	pai<u>l</u>s

3. ACCURACY/FLUENCY BUILDING For each column, have students say any underlined part, then read each word. Next, have them read the column.

A1 Mixed Practice	**B1** Mixed Practice	**C1** Related Words	**D1** Tricky Words	**E1** Tricky Words
t<u>oa</u>ds	destr<u>oy</u>	protect	special	although
foll<u>ow</u>	<u>c</u>enter	protects	movement	group
cr<u>aw</u>l	p<u>oi</u>son	protected	break	toward
fas<u>c</u>inate	c<u>au</u>se	protecting	climbed	actually
thr<u>ea</u>ds	lar<u>ge</u>	protection	certain	usually

4. WORD ENDINGS Have students read the underlined word, then the word with an ending.

Ⓐ	<u>smart</u>est	<u>smell</u>ing	<u>desert</u>s
Ⓑ	<u>garden</u>s	<u>branch</u>es	<u>reason</u>s

5. MORPHOGRAPHS AND AFFIXES Have students read the underlined word part, then the word.

danger<u>ous</u>	<u>dis</u>play	vibra<u>tion</u>	<u>be</u>cause

8

FOCUS LESSON
Skills and Strategies

REPORT WRITING

PURPOSE

This lesson provides explicit instruction in how to use research notes to write the body and ending of a report. The lesson prepares students for Comprehension and Skill Work.

COMPREHENSION PROCESSES

Understand, Apply, Evaluate, Create

PROCEDURES

1 REVIEW THE INTRODUCTION

- Have students read the introduction written during yesterday's Focus Lesson.

  Everyone, let's read the introduction we wrote yesterday. (Spiders are . . .)

- Using an overhead projection or enlarged copy of the introduction, say something like:

  Today, we're going to work on writing the body of the report and the conclusion.

2 BODY OF THE REPORT: TOPICS 1 and 2

Locating Information; Using Vocabulary—carnivore; Responding; Generating Ideas

- Introduce the first topic. Say something like:

  Let's read the example in our Focus Lesson. Read the direction for the first topic. (Select a topic. Complete . . .) This example was written using research notes on spiderwebs.

  Everyone, read the example. (One of the most interesting things about . . .)

  Did the topic sentence tell what the paragraph was going to be about? (yes)

  What was the paragraph about? (spiderwebs)

  Did the example include at least two facts about spiderwebs? (yes)

  What were the facts? (Spiders spin sticky webs so they can catch insects . . .)

- Guide practice as students work on the second topic. Say something like:

  Now, we're going to work together and write about a second topic.

  Read the directions. (Select a second topic . . .) Let's write about what spiders eat.

- Have students look in their notes and then brainstorm about how to complete the topic sentence. Say something like:

  Look in your notes for information on what spiders eat. When you know how you might like to complete the topic sentence, put one finger on your nose.

  [Tony], how might we start to complete the topic sentence? (Another interesting . . .)

  Those are all great ways to start a paragraph! I'm going to write . . .

  Complete the topic sentence by writing "the way they eat."

- Have students use their notes to find other interesting facts about how spiders eat. Guide students as they compose the remainder of the paragraph.

  We need to explain why the way spiders eat is interesting. I wonder if we should explain that they are meat eaters. What would be a snazzy way to write that? (Spiders are carnivores.)

  Excellent. Let's write how spiders catch and eat their prey. What happens first . . .

PREP NOTES

To demonstrate how to write a report, use an overhead of pages 9 and 10 in student *Exercise Book 3*, write on a transparency placed over the page, or use a paper copy.

RESEARCH NOTES

Students will need their research notes to complete this Focus Lesson.

PACING

Focus Lessons 6b and 6c should take 15 to 20 minutes. There is no Story Reading on this day to allow students additional time to work on their reports.

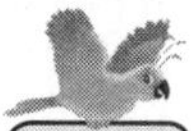

FOCUS LESSON Skills and Strategies

Body of the Report

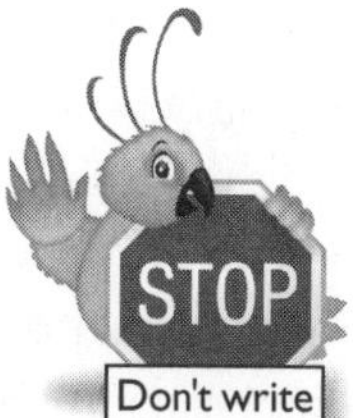

STOP

Don't write in your Exercise Book.

■ **1ST TOPIC** • Select a topic. Complete the topic sentence. Then write at least two facts about the topic.

One of the most interesting things about spiders is _the webs they spin._ Spiders spin sticky webs so they can catch insects. Spiders don't get stuck in their sticky webs because they have an oil on their bodies to keep them from sticking.

■ **2ND TOPIC** • Select a second topic. Complete the topic sentence. Then write at least three facts about the topic.

Another interesting thing about spiders is _the way they eat._ Spiders are carnivores. They catch insects. Then they use poison in their fangs to kill them. Spiders can't chew so they turn the insects into liquid and slurp them up.

Blackline Master **9**

REPORT WRITING *(continued)*

3 CONCLUSION OF THE REPORT

Using Vocabulary—respectful

- Have students read the directions.

  Read the first direction for writing the ending or conclusion to the report.
  (Write a paragraph that tells your reader how you feel about spiders.
  You may want to end your report with what else you'd like to learn.
  Then draw a picture in the box.)
  Writing the conclusion will be easy. We need to think about how we feel about spiders. I know
  I've changed my mind. I used to think spiders were kind of yucky. Now I think they are awesome.

- Have students brainstorm with the group or in partners ways to complete the first sentence.
  Say something like:

  Everyone, think of a way to end the first sentence that tells how you feel about spiders or even
  how you will treat them. Thumbs up when you've thought how you would like to complete the
  first sentence.

  Partner 1, think and talk with your partner about how you would complete the
  first sentence.

  After 30 seconds, say something like: Partner 2, think and talk with your
  partner about how you would complete the first sentence.

  After 30 seconds, say something like: What did you come up with? (Now
  that I know more about spiders, I will be careful not to disturb a web because
  spiders work very hard to make them. Now that I know some spiders, I will
  never step on one again . . .)

> **PARTNER THINK AND TALK**
>
> Having partners share ideas with one another keeps active engagement high. Consider using Partner Think and Talks as time allows.

  Those are all wonderful ways to start your ending. Save those ideas for your own report. I think
  I'll write, "Now that I know more about spiders, I will try to be more respectful of them."

  After the sentence starter, write "will try to be more respectful of them."

  Hmmm . . . I like that sentence because it has a snazzy word—*respectful*.
  There's more space, so what should I do? (Write more.)
  Yes, I need to think about ways to write more about being respectful of spiders. So I think I'll
  write a question: "Did you know that spiders help people?" Then I'll be clever and explain how
  spiders help people. I'll write "They help people by eating insects."

  After the sentence starter, write "Did you know that spiders help people? They help people by eating insects."

  What else did the directions tell us to write? (what else we'd like to learn)
  Let's look at the pictures in our book. We might get some ideas.

  What would you like to learn more about? (I'd like to learn more about the spiders that are as big
  as dinner plates. I wonder what they eat.)

- Have students read the concluding paragraph. Remind them that they will get to use all their
  good ideas in their own reports during independent work.

  This is a wonderful group report. I think your reports are going to be even better. I can't wait to
  read them. I know that each one will be unique!

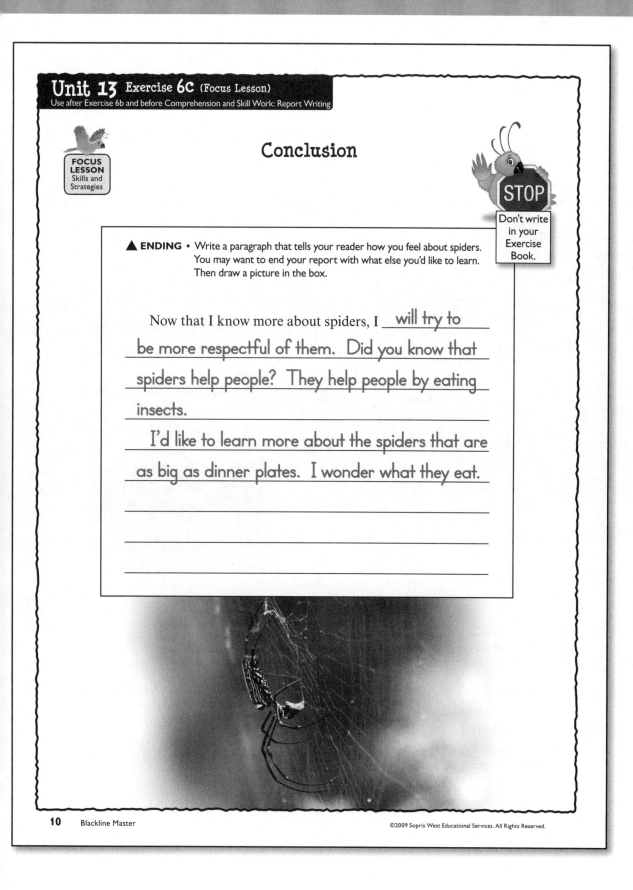

Unit 13 Exercise **6C** (Focus Lesson)

Use after Exercise 6b and before Comprehension and Skill Work: Report Writing

FOCUS
LESSON
Skills and
Strategies

Conclusion

STOP

Don't write
in your
Exercise
Book.

▲ **ENDING** • Write a paragraph that tells your reader how you feel about spiders. You may want to end your report with what else you'd like to learn. Then draw a picture in the box.

Now that I know more about spiders, I __will try to__ be more respectful of them. Did you know that spiders help people? They help people by eating insects.

I'd like to learn more about the spiders that are as big as dinner plates. I wonder what they eat.

BODY OF THE REPORT

COMPREHENSION PROCESSES

Remember, Understand, Apply, Create

WRITING TRAITS

Ideas and Content
Organization—Topic,
Supporting Details
Word Choice
Conventions—Complete Sentence,
Capital, Period
Presentation

Identifying—Topic, Facts
Summarizing—Facts
(Supporting Details); Explaining
Sentence Writing; Paragraph Writing
Sentence Completion

Identifying—Topic, Facts
Summarizing—Facts
(Supporting Details); Explaining
Sentence Writing; Paragraph Writing
Sentence Completion

Spider, Spider, on the Wall

Unit 13 Report Writing   Body (3 of 4)

■ **1ST TOPIC** • Select a topic. Complete the topic sentence. Then write at least two facts about the topic.
(Accept any reasonable response.)
One of the most interesting things about spiders is   the splendid
webs they make. Some webs look like a funnel. Some webs
are kind of a mess of silk. Other webs have spokes like a
bicycle tire. Spiders use their beautiful webs to trap food.

> **Note**
> In this sample, the student used notes from the matrix on page 3 to construct her paragraph. She also added words to make her paragraph more interesting.

■ **2ND TOPIC** • Select a second topic. Complete the topic sentence. Then write at least three facts about the topic.

Another interesting thing about spiders is   how they make their
webs. They have spinnerets that make liquid silk. When
spiders spin their webs, the silk thread is very thin but stronger
than steel.

©2009 Sopris West Educational Services. All Rights Reserved.   11

PROCEDURES

For each step, demonstrate and guide practice, if needed. Then have students complete the page independently.

Note: Students will use their Unit 13 Research Notes (Note Taking 1–4) to complete this activity.

1. **Report Writing: Body of the Report—Specific Instructions**
   • Have students get out their Unit 13 Research Notes (Note Taking 1–4). Remind students they will use their notes to complete the body of their report. (See Exercise 6b.)
   • Have students use their notes to write two fact summary paragraphs.

CONCLUSION

Generating Ideas—Conclusion
Summarizing—Facts
(Supporting Details); Explaining
Sentence Completion
Sentence Writing; Paragraph Writing

Visualizing, Illustrating

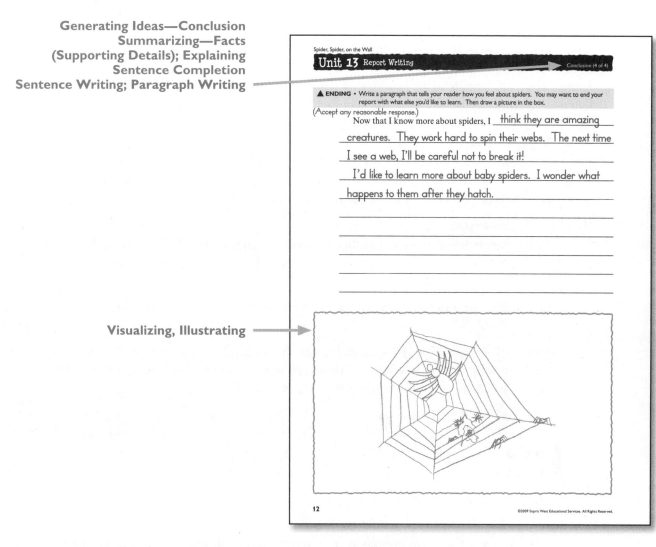

Spider, Spider, on the Wall

Unit 13 Report Writing — Conclusion (4 of 4)

▲ **ENDING** • Write a paragraph that tells your reader how you feel about spiders. You may want to end your report with what else you'd like to learn. Then draw a picture in the box.

(Accept any reasonable response.)

Now that I know more about spiders, I think they are amazing creatures. They work hard to spin their webs. The next time I see a web, I'll be careful not to break it!

I'd like to learn more about baby spiders. I wonder what happens to them after they hatch.

12 ©2009 Sopris West Educational Services. All Rights Reserved.

2. **Report Writing: Conclusion, Illustrating—Specific Instructions**
   - Have students write a conclusion. Remind students that they can end with the most interesting thing they learned about spiders and/or a sentence about what they would still like to learn.
   - Have students illustrate their report.

① SOUND REVIEW

Use selected Sound Cards from Units 1–13.

② SOUND PRACTICE

- For each task, have students spell and say the focus sound in the gray bar. For the Bossy <u>E</u>, read the header.
- Next, have students read each underlined sound, the word, then the whole column.
- Repeat with each column, building accuracy first, then fluency.

③ ACCURACY AND FLUENCY BUILDING

- For each task, have students say any underlined part, then read the word.
- Set a pace. Then have students read the whole words in each task and column.
- Provide repeated practice, building accuracy first, then fluency.

B1. Compound Words

Have students tell you what a compound word is, then have students read the words.

A compound word is made of two . . . (small words). Read the compound words.

C1. Reading by Analogy

Have students figure out how to say *wa-* by reading other words they know.

E1. Tricky Words

- For each Tricky Word, have students use the sounds and word parts they know to silently sound out the word. Use the word in a sentence to help with pronunciation.
- If the word is unfamiliar, tell students the word.

create	Sue likes to paint pictures. She likes to . . . *create* . . . art.
creator	The one who painted the picture was the . . . *creator* . . . of the art.
blood	Hospitals depend on people to donate . . . *blood.*
usually	What you do most of the time is what you . . . *usually* . . . do.

- Have students go back and read the whole words in the column.

E2. Animal Names

- Tell students these are the names of animals they will read about in the story.
- Have students use the sounds and word parts they know to figure out the words. Use the words in sentences, as needed.

④ MULTISYLLABIC WORDS

For each word, have students read the syllables, then the whole word. Use the word in a sentence, as appropriate.

sparkled	The shiny diamonds . . . *sparkled.*
permission	If we want to leave the classroom, we must ask for . . . *permission.*
wiggled	The dog barked and . . . *wiggled* . . . its tail.
introduction	The first part of a book is sometimes called the . . . *introduction.*
amphibians	Frogs and toads are . . . *amphibians.*
metamorphosis	The tadpole turned into a frog. It went through a . . . *metamorphosis.*

⑤ MORPHOGRAPHS AND AFFIXES

⑥ GENERALIZATION: READING NEW WORDS IN PARAGRAPHS

- Have students read the paragraph silently, then out loud. Tell students to use the sounds and word parts they know to read any difficult words.
- Repeat practice, as needed.

Centipede and Grandmother Spider

Unit 13 Exercise 7a
Use before Exercise 7b

1. SOUND REVIEW Use selected Sound Cards from Units 1–13.

2. SOUND PRACTICE In each column, have students spell and say the sound, next say any underlined sound and the word, then read the column.

-le	a as in ago	Bossy E	e as in eagle
midd<u>le</u>	<u>a</u>wake	wh<u>a</u>le	<u>sea</u>s
chuck<u>le</u>	<u>a</u>round	sc<u>a</u>les	pl<u>ea</u>se
beet<u>le</u>	<u>a</u>dult	c<u>a</u>ves	cr<u>ea</u>ture

3. ACCURACY/FLUENCY BUILDING For each column, have students say any underlined part, then read each word. Next, have them read the column.

A1 Mixed Practice	B1 Compound Words	C1 Reading by Analogy	D1 Word Endings	E1 Tricky Words
plent<u>y</u>	grandfather	<u>wa</u>ter	<u>shiver</u>ed	create
shrimp	grasshopper	<u>wa</u>sp	<u>reptile</u>s	creator
g<u>oo</u>se	rattlesnake	s<u>wa</u>mps		blood
d<u>ew</u>	backbone	wig<u>wa</u>m	noise	usually
h<u>aw</u>k	dewdrops		noisy	
inst<u>ea</u>d		C2 Rhyming Words		E2 Animal Names
l<u>a</u>kes		lizard	crackle	Bear
		blizzard	crackling	Heron
		buzzard		Wolf

4. MULTISYLLABIC WORDS Have students read each word part, then read each whole word.

Ⓐ	spar•kled	sparkled	per•mis•sion	permission
Ⓑ	wig•gled	wiggled	in•tro•duc•tion	introduction
Ⓒ	am•phib•i•ans	amphibians	met•a•mor•pho•sis	metamorphosis

5. MORPHOGRAPHS AND AFFIXES Have students read each underlined part, then the word.

<u>dis</u>play	<u>ex</u>cited	close<u>ly</u>	moutain<u>ous</u>	ques<u>tion</u>

6. GENERALIZATION Have students read the paragraph silently, then out loud. (New words: homework, mosquito, beetle)

    Jane looked up from her homework as she waved away a mosquito buzzing around her head. "These winged insects are such pests," she thought. She went back to her homework, and soon a beetle crawled onto her desk. Just as she was about to catch the beetle, a lizard came and grabbed it. "Wow," said Jane. "Insects and a cold-blooded reptile. What an interesting night of homework!"

TEACH TO MASTERY/ DISCRIMINATION PRACTICE

Repeated Practice (Reminder)

Provide repeated practice on each task. If you hear an error, gently correct the whole group with a demonstration and/or guided practice. Move to another skill or task, then return to the difficult item many times—mixing group and individual turns, independent of your voice. When a task is easy, build speed of recognition.

Remember, practice makes perfect! And practice builds fluency.

11

MAZE READING

PURPOSE

The purpose of this lesson is to provide explicit instruction in how to complete a Maze Reading exercise. This will prepare students for future Comprehension and Skill Work and will also provide students with practice on a maze test-taking format. Students do not write in their books but will watch and respond as you guide them through the lesson.

PREP NOTE

To demonstrate how to complete the maze activity, use an overhead of page 12 in student *Exercise Book 3*, write on a transparency placed over the page, or use a paper copy.

COMPREHENSION PROCESSES

Understand

PROCEDURES

1 INTRODUCTION

Explain the purpose of the lesson and how students will learn a strategy for selecting the correct word to complete the sentences in the maze comprehension exercise. Say something like:

Today, we are going to learn how to complete a Maze Reading. A maze is a puzzle.

So this exercise is a puzzle for you. As you read, you'll need to stop and pick the best of three words to complete some of the sentences. If you pick the wrong word, the sentence won't make sense.

2 MAZE READING

Comprehension Monitoring, Test Taking

• Guide practice in selecting the best word to complete the paragraph.

Look at the first box. Read the first sentence.

(Even though spider silk is very strong, spiderwebs can wear out.)

The next sentence is tricky. Read the first part and stop at the parentheses.

(A big insect can punch a . . .)

The sentence stops, so now we get to choose the next word.

There are three choices. Let's try reading the whole sentence with the first choice.

A big insect can punch a . . . *boy* right through a web.

Does "punch a *boy* right through a web" make sense? (no)

Let's try reading the sentence with just the second word. Read with me.

A big insect can punch a . . . *hardens* right through a web.

Does "hardens right through a web" make sense? (no) No, that sentence doesn't make sense.

Try reading the sentence with the last word. Read with me.

A big insect can punch a . . . *hole* right through a web.

Does that sentence make sense? (yes)

I'll circle the word *hole*.

Repeat with each sentence. If the answer is the first or second word, have students continue on to the next sentence if they are sure it makes sense. If they aren't sure, try each possible answer.

• Have students read the whole passage to make sure it makes sense.

Let's read the whole passage to make sure it makes sense. Read the circled word when you get to the parentheses. (Even though spider silk is very strong, spider webs can wear out. A big insect can punch a hole right through the web . . .)

Centipede and Grandmother Spider

Unit 13 Exercise **7b** (Focus Lesson)
Use after Exercise 7a and before the Introduction and Chapter 1

FOCUS
LESSON
Skills and
Strategies

Maze Reading

STOP
Don't write
in your
Exercise
Book.

1 Read!

Even though spider silk is very strong, spiderwebs can wear out.
A big insect can punch a (boy, hardens, hole) right through a web.
After a (dollar, provides, night) of hunting, many spiders eat their
(which, water, webs). Then they rest all day and (tumble, build,
instead) a new one in the evening.

2 Think! Does it make sense?

- A big insect can punch a (**boy**, hardens, hole) right through a web.
- A big insect can punch a (boy, **hardens**, hole) right through a web.
- A big insect can punch a (boy, hardens, **hole**) right through a web.

3 You try it!

After a (dollar, provides, night) of hunting, many spiders eat their
(which, water, webs).

What makes sense?

4 Now try the whole Maze Reading in the top box.

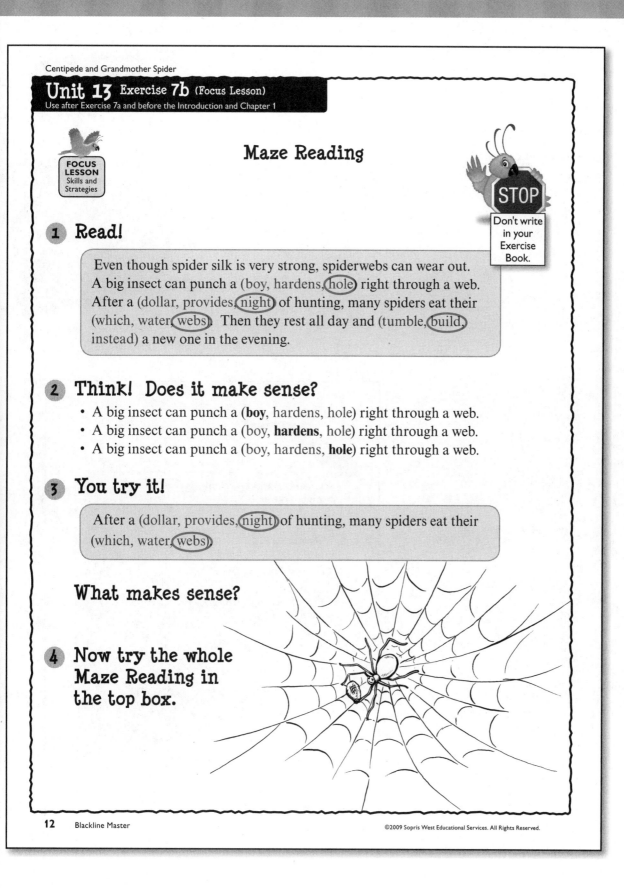

COMPREHENSION PROCESSES

Remember, Apply

PROCEDURES

1. Reviewing the Table of Contents

Using Table of Contents

Have students find the Table of Contents and the title page for "Centipede and Grandmother Spider." Next, have students turn to page 38.

2. Introducing the Story

Identifying—Title; Inferring— Main Characters

- Discuss the title and main characters. Say something like:

  What's the title of this story? (Centipede and Grandmother Spider)

  Who do you think the main characters in this story are?

  (Centipede and Grandmother Spider)

- Read the gray text and discuss the questions.

Centipede and Grandmother Spider
by Bailey Phelps
illustrated by Karen Perrins

American Indians have a *tradition* of passing stories down from one generation to the next. These stories are called legends. What are the stories called? **1**
Who has a tradition of passing stories on from generation to generation? **2**

38

❶ **Remember:** Identifying—What; Using Vocabulary— legend (The stories are called legends.)

❷ **Remember:** Identifying—Who (American Indians have a tradition of passing stories down from generation to generation.)

COMPREHENSION PROCESSES

Understand, Apply

PROCEDURES

Introducing Vocabulary

> **permission, reptile ☆ amphibian**

- For each vocabulary word, have students read the word by parts, then read the whole word.
- Read the student-friendly explanations to students as they follow with their fingers. Then have students use the vocabulary word by following the gray text.
- Review and discuss the photos and illustrations.

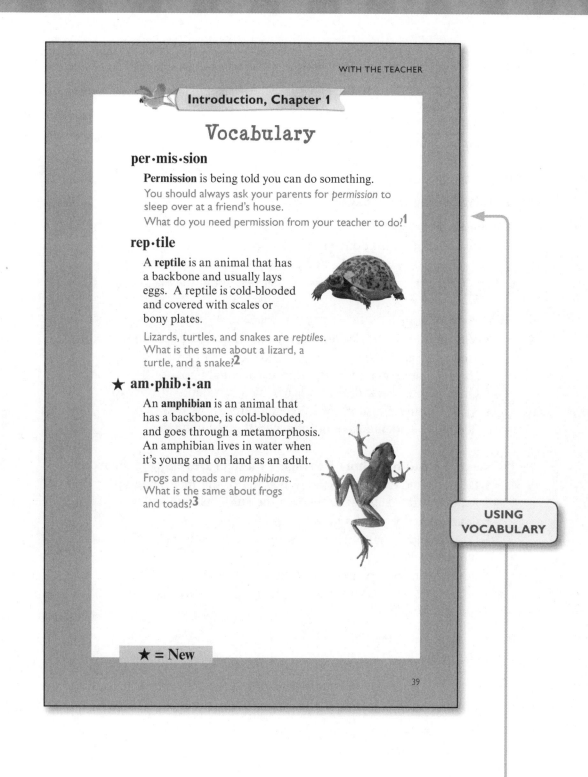

WITH THE TEACHER

Introduction, Chapter 1

Vocabulary

per·mis·sion

Permission is being told you can do something.

You should always ask your parents for permission to sleep over at a friend's house.

What do you need permission from your teacher to do?[1]

rep·tile

A **reptile** is an animal that has a backbone and usually lays eggs. A reptile is cold-blooded and covered with scales or bony plates.

Lizards, turtles, and snakes are reptiles. What is the same about a lizard, a turtle, and a snake?[2]

★ am·phib·i·an

An **amphibian** is an animal that has a backbone, is cold-blooded, and goes through a metamorphosis. An amphibian lives in water when it's young and on land as an adult.

Frogs and toads are amphibians. What is the same about frogs and toads?[3]

★ = New

39

USING
VOCABULARY

❶ **Apply:** Using Vocabulary—permission (I need permission to leave the classroom.)

❷ **Understand:** Defining and Using Vocabulary—reptile (Lizards, turtles, and snakes all have a backbone, lay eggs, are cold-blooded, and are covered with scales or bony plates.)

❸ **Understand:** Defining and Using Vocabulary—amphibian, metamorphosis (Frogs and toads have backbones, are cold-blooded, and go through a metamorphosis. They also live in water and on land.)

INTRODUCTION INSTRUCTIONS

Students read the Introduction with the teacher and Chapter 1 on their own.

COMPREHENSION PROCESSES

Remember, Understand, Apply, Create

PROCEDURES

1. Introducing the Chapter

Identifying—Title

Explain what an introduction is. Say something like:

Turn to page 40. What's the title of this section? (Introduction)

This is a beginning part of the story that tells about the main story.

2. First Reading

- Ask questions and discuss the text as indicated by the gray text.
- Mix group and individual turns, independent of your voice.
  Have students work toward a group accuracy goal of 0–2 errors.
  Quietly keep track of errors made by all students in the group.
- After reading the story, practice any difficult words.
  Repeat, if students have not reached the accuracy goal.

3. Second Reading, Short Passage Practice: Developing Prosody

- Demonstrate expressive, fluent reading of the first paragraph.
  Read at a rate slightly faster than the students' rate.
- Guide practice with your voice.
- Provide individual turns while others track with their fingers and whisper read.
- Repeat with one paragraph or page at a time.

REPEATED READINGS

Prosody

On the second reading, students practice developing prosody— phrasing and expression. Research has shown that prosody is related to both fluency and comprehension.

CORRECTING DECODING ERRORS

During story reading, gently correct any error, then have students reread the sentence.

WITH THE TEACHER

Introduction

Gray Cloud woke up very early. He was excited. Today he would not have to help his mother. She had given him permission to visit his grandfather.

The sun was not yet up when Gray Cloud left his wigwam. He shivered a little in the cool air. He saw places where bright drops of dew sparkled in the early light. The drops were in straight lines. When Gray Cloud looked more closely, he saw that the lines were spiderwebs.

Gray Cloud saw that one web had trapped a small insect. He could see how the dewdrops shook when the little creature wiggled in the sticky web. He decided that he would ask Grandfather about insects and spiders.

Who is Gray Cloud?[1] Why did he decide to ask his grandfather about insects and spiders?[2]

40

COMPREHENDING AS YOU GO

[1] **Remember:** Identifying—Main Character (Gray Cloud is the main character. Gray Cloud is a young boy.)

[2] **Understand:** Explaining (He saw a small insect trapped in a spiderweb.)

CENTIPEDE AND GRANDMOTHER SPIDER

41

WITH THE TEACHER

Gray Cloud made his way to Grandfather's wigwam. He heard the crackling of burning wood inside, so he knew Grandfather had started his morning fire.

"Who is there?" came the voice from inside.

"It is Gray Cloud. I have come to visit."

"Come inside," chuckled the old man. Gray Cloud went into the wigwam and sat on the ground by the small fire. Then Grandfather asked, "What questions do you have for me today?"

"Grandfather," said Gray Cloud, "I was looking at spiderwebs this morning. Tell me, do spiders stay awake all night?"

"Most of them do," said the old man. "They have to work hard to catch insects for their food."

"Tell me, Grandfather," the boy went on. "Why does Spider stay up all night? Why does Spider make webs instead of hunting like Wolf or Bear? Why does she eat insects?"

What questions did Gray Cloud have for his grandfather?[1]

42

COMPREHENDING AS YOU GO

1 Understand: Summarizing (Gray Cloud asked why spiders stay up all night. He asked why spiders make webs and why they eat insects.)

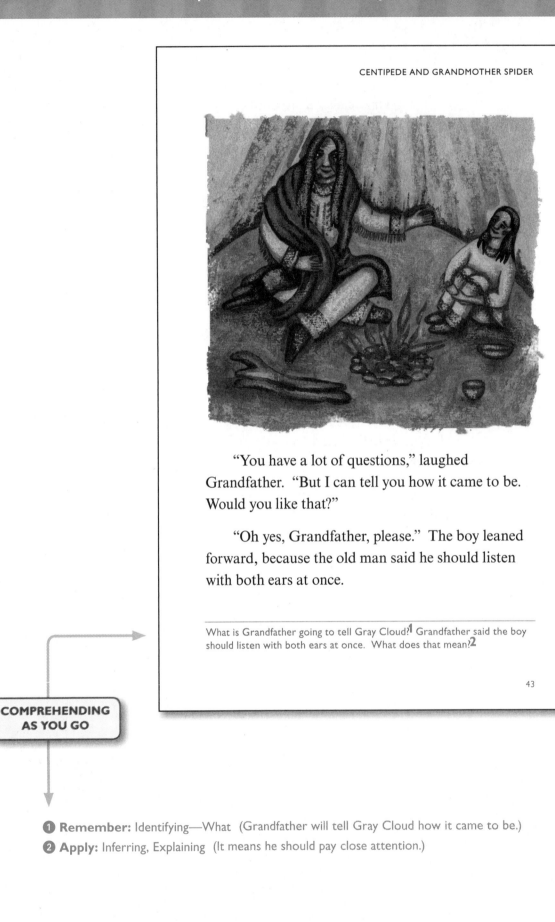

CENTIPEDE AND GRANDMOTHER SPIDER

"You have a lot of questions," laughed Grandfather. "But I can tell you how it came to be. Would you like that?"

"Oh yes, Grandfather, please." The boy leaned forward, because the old man said he should listen with both ears at once.

What is Grandfather going to tell Gray Cloud?**1** Grandfather said the boy should listen with both ears at once. What does that mean?**2**

43

COMPREHENDING
AS YOU GO

1 **Remember:** Identifying—What (Grandfather will tell Gray Cloud how it came to be.)
2 **Apply:** Inferring, Explaining (It means he should pay close attention.)

Grandfather began in this way:

Long, long ago, back in the very beginning, Creator was making the world. Creator made tall mountains and low places. There were deserts filled with sand. There were forests filled with trees. There were seas and lakes and rivers. There were flat places covered with grass. There were swamps filled with mud and a little water.

Mountains

Deserts

Forests

Seas

44

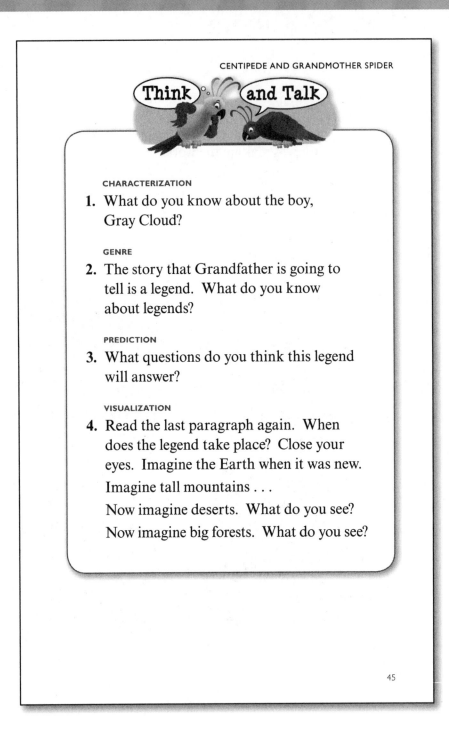

CENTIPEDE AND GRANDMOTHER SPIDER

Think and Talk

CHARACTERIZATION

1. What do you know about the boy, Gray Cloud?

GENRE

2. The story that Grandfather is going to tell is a legend. What do you know about legends?

PREDICTION

3. What questions do you think this legend will answer?

VISUALIZATION

4. Read the last paragraph again. When does the legend take place? Close your eyes. Imagine the Earth when it was new.

   Imagine tall mountains . . .

   Now imagine deserts. What do you see?

   Now imagine big forests. What do you see?

45

❶ **Understand:** Describing—Character Traits (Characterization); Using Vocabulary—curious (Gray Cloud is a young, curious boy.)

❷ **Understand:** Explaining—Genre; Using Vocabulary—generation, legend (Legends are stories that are passed down from one generation to the next.)

❸ **Apply:** Predicting (It will answer the questions "Why does Spider stay up all night? Why does Spider make webs instead of hunt? Why does she eat insects?")

❹ **Understand:** Visualizing, Describing (I see big sand dunes. I see enormous pine trees . . .)

CHAPTER 1 INSTRUCTIONS

Students read without the teacher, independently or with partners.

COMPREHENSION PROCESSES

Remember, Understand, Create

PROCEDURES FOR READING ON YOUR OWN

1. Getting Ready

Have students turn to page 46.

2. Setting a Purpose

Identifying—Title, Setting; Explaining; Describing

Before students begin reading, say something like:

Read the title of this chapter. (A Mountain Full of Animals)

Read to find out the answers to these questions:

- When does the story take place?
- Why did the animals live in the mountain?
- What did the inside of the mountain look like?

> **PREP NOTE**
>
> **Setting a Purpose**
> Write questions on a chalkboard, white board, or large piece of paper before working with your small group.

3. Reading on Your Own: Partner or Whisper Reading

- Have students take turns reading every other page with a partner or have students whisper read on their own.
- Continue having students track each word with their fingers.
- Have students ask themselves or their partners the gray text questions.

4. Comprehension and Skill Work

Tell students they will do Comprehension and Skill Activities 5 and 6 after they read Chapter 1. Guide practice, as needed. For teacher directions, see pages 105 and 106.

5. Homework 6: Repeated Reading

Chapter 1

A Mountain Full of Animals

Long, long ago, back in the very beginning, Creator was making the world. Creator made tall mountains and low places. There were deserts filled with sand. There were forests with trees. There were seas and lakes and rivers. There were flat places covered with grass. There were swamps filled with mud and a little water.

In the middle of the world was a very big mountain. In that mountain were all the different kinds of animals that would live in all those places Creator had made. There were great big caves inside the mountain.

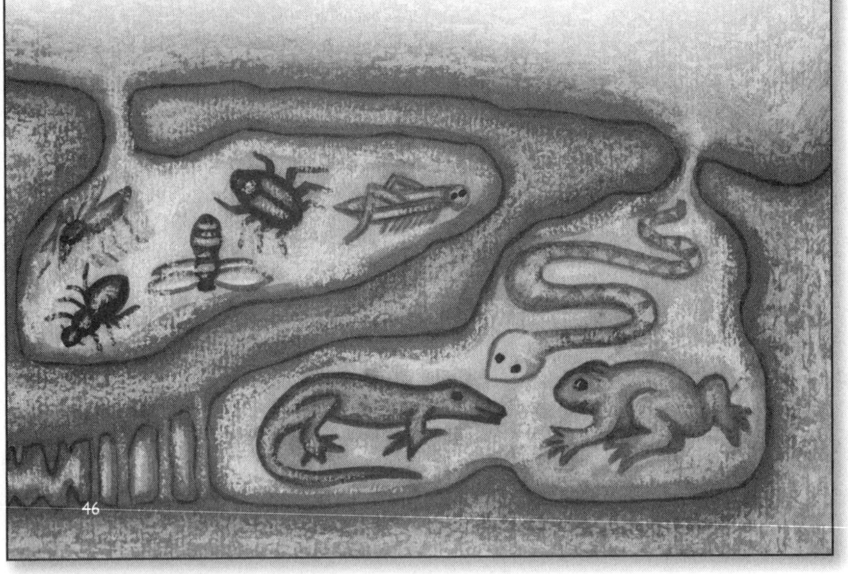

46

CENTIPEDE AND GRANDMOTHER SPIDER

At the top of the mountain was a big cave for the Winged Ones, the birds. On one side was water, where Duck and Goose and Heron splashed around. At the other end was a high roof so Hawk and Eagle and Buzzard had plenty of room to fly.

There was a cave for reptiles and amphibians. It was wet on one side and dry on the other. Rattlesnake, Lizard, Frog, and many others crawled or hopped or ran around on the floor of the cave.

Describe the world that Creator was making. What did it look like and who lived there?[1]

47

COMPREHENDING
AS YOU GO

❶ **Understand:** Describing—What, Who (The world had tall mountains and low places, deserts and forests, and seas and rivers. It had a big mountain in the middle where all the different animals lived.)

ON YOUR OWN

There was a special cave for the insects. Grasshopper was there. Ant, Beetle, Wasp, and Mosquito were there.

At the bottom of the mountain was a cave for the creatures that lived in water. In it were Fish, Crab, Shrimp, and even great big Whale!

All of the caves were very noisy. The animals were excited. Soon they would go out into the world where they would have homes of their own.

Why were the animals excited?[1] If you were a big bear and you could choose your own home, where would it be?[2] If you were a huge whale and you could choose your own home, where would it be?[3]

48

COMPREHENDING AS YOU GO

❶ **Understand:** Explaining (The animals were excited because they would soon go out into the world and get their own homes.)

❷ **Create:** Generating Ideas (If I were a bear, I'd choose a nice big cave near lots of berry bushes . . .)

❸ **Create:** Generating Ideas (If I were a whale, I would want to live in a big ocean with lots of fish to eat . . .)

STORY COMPREHENSION

COMPREHENSION PROCESSES

Remember, Understand, Apply

WRITING TRAITS

Conventions—Period

Identifying—Genre
Defining and Using Vocabulary—legend

Identifying—Narrator

Identifying—Setting

Identifying—What

Explaining

Inferring
Using Vocabulary—legend

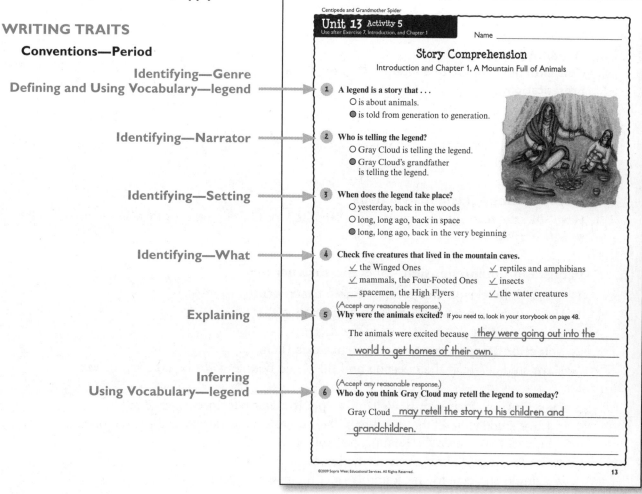

Centipede and Grandmother Spider

Unit 13 Activity 5
Use after Exercise 7, Introduction, and Chapter 1

Name _____

Story Comprehension
Introduction and Chapter 1, A Mountain Full of Animals

1. A legend is a story that . . .
   ○ is about animals.
   ● is told from generation to generation.

2. Who is telling the legend?
   ○ Gray Cloud is telling the legend.
   ● Gray Cloud's grandfather is telling the legend.

3. When does the legend take place?
   ○ yesterday, back in the woods
   ○ long, long ago, back in space
   ● long, long ago, back in the very beginning

4. Check five creatures that lived in the mountain caves.
   ✓ the Winged Ones   ✓ reptiles and amphibians
   ✓ mammals, the Four-Footed Ones   ✓ insects
   __ spacemen, the High Flyers   ✓ the water creatures

   (Accept any reasonable response.)

5. Why were the animals excited? If you need to, look in your storybook on page 48.

   The animals were excited because _they were going out into the_
   world to get homes of their own.

   (Accept any reasonable response.)

6. Who do you think Gray Cloud may retell the legend to someday?

   Gray Cloud _may retell the story to his children and_
   grandchildren.

13

PROCEDURES

For each step, demonstrate and guide practice, as needed. Then have students complete the page independently.

1. **Selection Response—Basic Instructions** (Items 1–4)
   Have students read the question, then fill in the bubble or check the blank with the correct answer.

2. **Sentence Completion—Basic Instructions** (Items 5, 6)
   Have students read the sentence starters, then fill in the blanks to complete the sentences. Remind students to put a period at the end of the sentence.

Self-monitoring
Have students check and correct their work.

MAZE READING AND PARAGRAPH COMPREHENSION

COMPREHENSION PROCESSES
Remember, Understand

WRITING TRAITS
Word Choice
Conventions—Complete Sentence, Capital, Period
Presentation

PROCEDURES
For each step, demonstrate and guide practice, as needed. Then have students complete the page independently.

Maze Reading—Basic Instructions
Have students read the sentences and select the word in parentheses that best completes the sentence. Have students circle the word.

Paragraph Comprehension—Specific Instructions

1. **Yes/No: Selection Response—Basic Instructions** (Item 1)
   Have students reread the passage and circle yes or no.

2. **Selection Response—Basic Instructions** (Item 2)
   Have students read the question and fill in the bubble with the correct answer.

3. **Description: Paragraph Writing—Specific Instructions** (Item 3)
   • Have students read the directions, then write a short descriptive paragraph using at least two sentences. Remind students to use a snazzy word.
   • Guide students through the activity, only as needed.
   • Remind students to check and correct their work.

Comprehension Monitoring Test Taking

Comprehension Monitoring

Defining

Describing

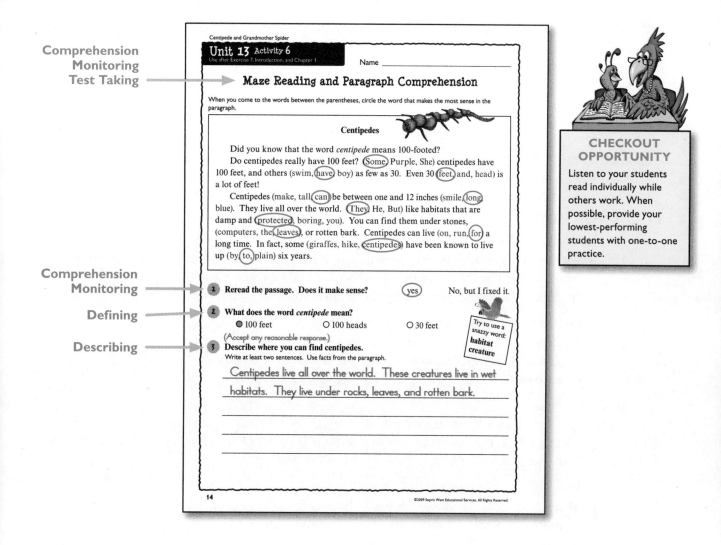

Centipede and Grandmother Spider

Unit 13 Activity 6
Use after Exercise 7, Introduction, and Chapter 1

Name _____

Maze Reading and Paragraph Comprehension

When you come to the words between the parentheses, circle the word that makes the most sense in the paragraph.

Centipedes

Did you know that the word *centipede* means 100-footed?

Do centipedes really have 100 feet? (**Some**, Purple, She) centipedes have 100 feet, and others (swim, **have**, boy) as few as 30. Even 30 (**feet**, and, head) is a lot of feet!

Centipedes (make, tall, **can**) be between one and 12 inches (smile, **long**, blue). They live all over the world. (**They**, He, But) like habitats that are damp and (**protected**, boring, you). You can find them under stones, (computers, the, **leaves**), or rotten bark. Centipedes can live (on, run, **for**) a long time. In fact, some (giraffes, hike, **centipedes**) have been known to live up (by, **to**, plain) six years.

---

1. **Reread the passage. Does it make sense?** (**yes**) No, but I fixed it.

2. **What does the word *centipede* mean?**
   ● 100 feet   ○ 100 heads   ○ 30 feet
   (Accept any reasonable response.)

   Try to use a snazzy word: **habitat creature**

3. **Describe where you can find centipedes.**
   Write at least two sentences. Use facts from the paragraph.

   Centipedes live all over the world. These creatures live in wet
   habitats. They live under rocks, leaves, and rotten bark.
   _____
   _____
   _____

14

① SOUND REVIEW

Have students read the sounds and key word phrases. Work for accuracy, then fluency.

② SHIFTY WORD BLENDING

For each word, have students say the underlined sound. Then have them sound out the word smoothly and say it. Use the words in sentences, as appropriate.

③ ACCURACY AND FLUENCY BUILDING

- For each task, have students say any underlined part, then read the word.
- Set a pace. Then have students read the whole words in each task and column.
- Provide repeated practice, building accuracy first, then fluency.

C1. Multisyllabic Words

- For the list of words divided by syllables, have students read each syllable, then the whole word. Use the word in a sentence, as appropriate.
- For the list of whole words, build accuracy and then fluency.

beetle	A ladybug is a type of . . . *beetle.*
cricket	An insect that looks like a grasshopper is a . . . *cricket.*
fictional	The character wasn't real. She was . . . *fictional.*
centipede	A kind of bug that has segments and lots of legs is a . . . *centipede.*

E1. Tricky Words

- For each Tricky Word, have students use the sounds and word parts they know to silently sound out the word. Use the word in a sentence to help with pronunciation.
- If the word is unfamiliar, tell students the word.

idea	The inventor had a great . . . *idea.*
able	The dog broke his leg, so he wasn't . . . *able* . . . to run.
music	Rock and roll is her favorite type of . . . *music.*
enough	She said, "I can't eat any more. I've had . . . *enough.*"
special	Sometimes, it's nice to feel . . . *special.*
create	What did you . . . *create?*
creator	An inventor created the light bulb. He was the . . . *creator.*

- Have students go back and read the whole words in the column.

④ READING BY ANALOGY

Have students figure out how to say *wa-* by reading words they already know.

⑤ MORPHOGRAPHS AND AFFIXES

- Have students read the underlined part, then the word.
- Repeat practice with whole words, mixing group and individual turns. Build accuracy, then fluency.

⑥ GENERALIZATION: READING NEW WORDS IN PARAGRAPHS

- Have students read the paragraph silently, then out loud. Tell students to use the sounds and word parts they know to read any difficult words.
- Repeat practice, as needed.

Centipede and Grandmother Spider

Unit 13 Exercise 8
Use before Chapters 2 and 3

1. SOUND REVIEW Have students review sounds for accuracy, then for fluency.

A	ph as in phone	u_e as in flute	ew as in crew	o_e as in bone	i as in silence
B	a_e	gi	oi	aw	-dge

2. SHIFTY WORD BLENDING For each word, have students say the underlined part, sound out smoothly, then read the word.

bl<u>ew</u>	<u>kn</u>ew	<u>kn</u>ee	<u>kn</u>eel	<u>wh</u>eel

3. ACCURACY/FLUENCY BUILDING For each column, have students say any underlined part, then read each word. Next, have them read the column.

A1 Mixed Practice	**B1** Bossy E	**C1** Multisyllabic Words	**D1** Word Endings	**E1** Tricky Words
belly	h<u>i</u>des	bee•tle	<u>eat</u>en	idea
f<u>air</u>	st<u>o</u>len	crick•et	<u>branch</u>es	able
sn<u>or</u>es	surv<u>i</u>ve	fic•tion•al	<u>visit</u>ed	music
c<u>au</u>se	**B2** Related Words	cen•ti•pede	<u>digg</u>ing	enough
g<u>i</u>ant	practice	beetle	<u>hopp</u>ing	special
threads	practicing	cricket	wiggle	create
legend	practiced	fictional	wiggling	creator
ton<u>igh</u>t		centipede		

4. READING BY ANALOGY Have students figure out how to pronounce the underlined word parts by reading words they already know.

w<u>a</u>ter	w<u>a</u>nder	w<u>a</u>sh	W<u>a</u>sp

5. MORPHOGRAPHS AND AFFIXES Have students read the underlined word part, then the word.

<u>un</u>happy	deep<u>ly</u>	<u>be</u>tween	<u>dis</u>appoint	ser<u>ious</u>

6. GENERALIZATION Have students read the paragraph silently, then out loud. (New words: honey, angry, obeyed)

Bzzz, bzzz, bzzz. Mike watched the little bee as it flew from flower to flower. The bee was working hard, taking juices from the flowers to make sweet, sticky honey. Mike reached out and touched the bee's wings. Uh, oh. That made the bee angry. As Mike ran away from the bee with a tear in his eye, he thought, "Mom told me to leave bees alone. I wish I had obeyed."

> **MIX IT UP (Reminder)**
>
> Response forms can be varied. Have students say the sounds using different rhythms. Have students use big voices, small voices, and deep voices. Pass the cards to students. Then have them find and return a sound. Be creative, but maintain a high rate of group responses.

COMPREHENSION PROCESSES

Understand, Apply

PROCEDURES

1. Introducing Vocabulary

★ obey ★ legend, creature

- For each vocabulary word, have students read the word by parts, then read the whole word.
- Read the student-friendly explanations to students as they follow with their fingers. Then have students use the vocabulary word by following the gray text.
- Review and discuss the photos and illustrations.

2. Now You Try It!

- Read or paraphrase the directions.
- Then have students read the word by parts, then read the whole word.
- Have students explain or define the word in their own words.
- Have students turn to the appropriate page in the glossary and discuss how their definition is the same as or different from the glossary's. Your students may like their definition better.

Note: By defining a word in their own words, students are demonstrating depth of word knowledge. Verbatim responses only demonstrate memorization. Encourage paraphrasing.

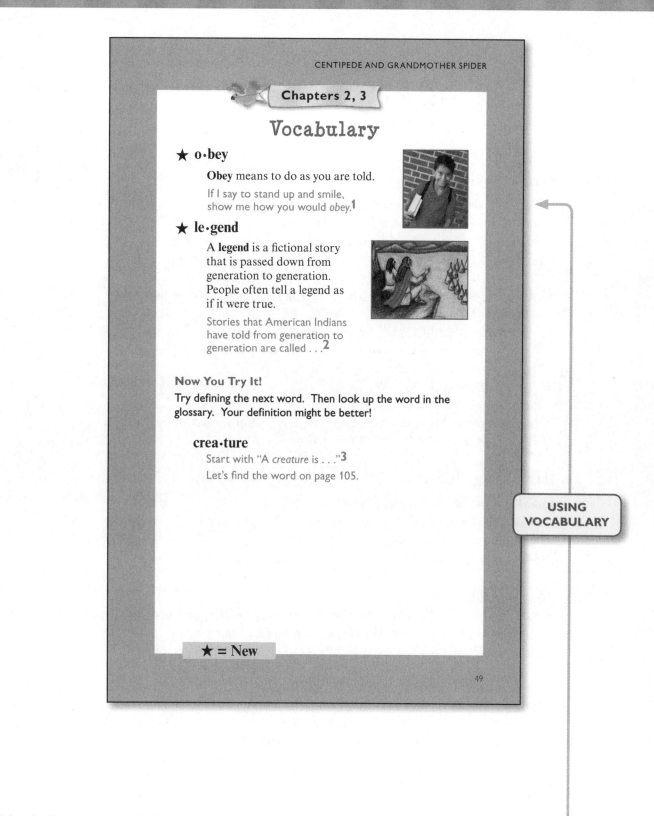

Chapters 2, 3

Vocabulary

★ **o·bey**

Obey means to do as you are told.

If I say to stand up and smile, show me how you would *obey*.[1]

★ **le·gend**

A **legend** is a fictional story that is passed down from generation to generation. People often tell a legend as if it were true.

Stories that American Indians have told from generation to generation are called . . .[2]

Now You Try It!

Try defining the next word. Then look up the word in the glossary. Your definition might be better!

crea·ture

Start with "A *creature* is . . ."[3]

Let's find the word on page 105.

★ = New

49

USING VOCABULARY

❶ **Apply:** Demonstrating; **Understand:** Using Vocabulary—obey

❷ **Understand:** Using Vocabulary—legend (legends)

❸ **Understand:** Defining and Using Vocabulary—creature; Using Glossary
(A creature is any living animal.)

CHAPTER 2 INSTRUCTIONS
Students read Chapter 2 with the teacher and Chapter 3 on their own.

COMPREHENSION PROCESSES
Remember, Understand, Apply

PROCEDURES

1. Reviewing Introduction and Chapter 1

Identifying—Main Characters, Setting; Explaining; Describing
- Have students turn to page 40. Quickly review who the main characters are and why Grandfather is telling the story.
- Have students turn to page 46. If time permits, have students reread Chapter 1 with you.
- Quickly discuss the questions from Chapter 1, Setting a Purpose. Say something like:

   Yesterday, you read Chapter 1 on your own. Let's see what you found out.
   When does the story take place? (The story takes place a long, long time ago, before there were animals in the world.)
   Why did the animals live in the mountain? (They were waiting to go into the world.)
   What did the inside of the mountain look like? (There were lots of caves, it was noisy, there were lots of different animals . . .)

2. Introducing Chapter 2

Identifying—Title; Inferring; Predicting
Discuss the title and main characters. Say something like:
What's the title of this chapter? (The Cave of Insects)
What kind of insects do you think we'll learn about? (ants, crickets, bees . . .)

3. First Reading
- Ask questions and discuss the text as indicated by the gray text.
- Mix group and individual turns, independent of your voice.
   Have students work toward a group accuracy goal of 0–5 errors.
   Quietly keep track of errors made by all students in the group.
- After reading the story, practice any difficult words.
   Repeat, if students have not reached the accuracy goal.

4. Second Reading, Timed Readings: Repeated Reading
- As time allows, have students do Timed Readings while others follow along.
- Time individuals for 30 seconds and encourage each child to work for a personal best.
- Determine words correct per minute. Record student scores.

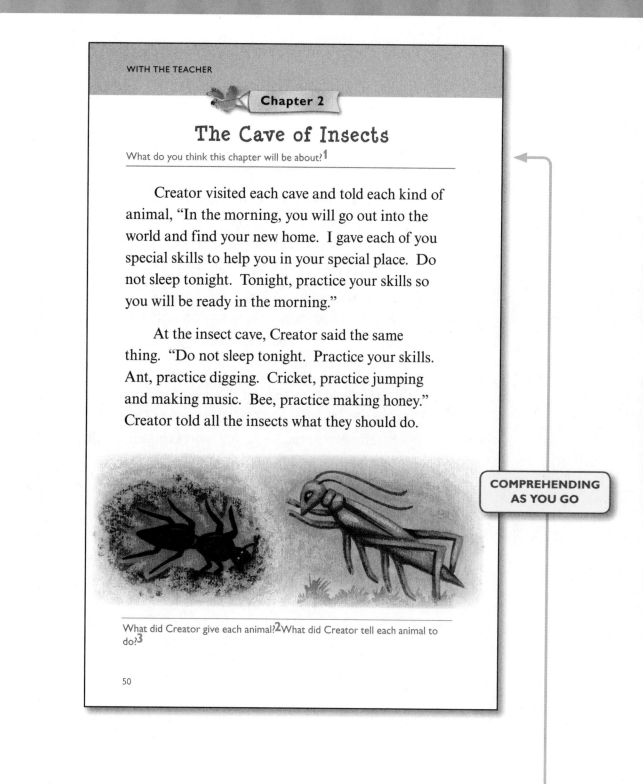

WITH THE TEACHER

Chapter 2

The Cave of Insects

What do you think this chapter will be about?[1]

Creator visited each cave and told each kind of animal, "In the morning, you will go out into the world and find your new home. I gave each of you special skills to help you in your special place. Do not sleep tonight. Tonight, practice your skills so you will be ready in the morning."

At the insect cave, Creator said the same thing. "Do not sleep tonight. Practice your skills. Ant, practice digging. Cricket, practice jumping and making music. Bee, practice making honey." Creator told all the insects what they should do.

What did Creator give each animal?[2] What did Creator tell each animal to do?[3]

50

COMPREHENDING AS YOU GO

❶ **Apply:** Predicting (It will be about the cave where the insects are.)

❷ **Remember:** Identifying—What (Creator gave each animal a special skill.)

❸ **Understand:** Explaining (Creator told the animals to practice their special skills so they would be ready in the morning.)

CENTIPEDE AND GRANDMOTHER SPIDER

In this time, the Old Ones say that all insects had eight legs. Creator had made them all that way. Ant had eight legs. Bee had eight legs. Wasp had eight legs, and Centipede had eight legs.

But Centipede was unhappy. He was so long and thin that his belly dragged on the ground between each pair of legs! "This is not fair," he said. "I am so long and thin. I should have more legs."

Centipede looked at the other insects. He thought, "They all have eight legs. But they are very small. They do not need all those legs. Six legs will be enough for them."

Centipede saw that the other insects were not doing what Creator had told them to do. They were going to sleep. Little tiny snores came from all around the cave. This gave Centipede an idea.

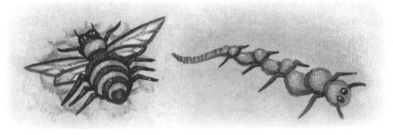

What was Centipede's problem?[1] What were the animals supposed to be doing?[2] What were they doing instead?[3] What do you think Centipede will do?[4]

51

COMPREHENDING
AS YOU GO

❶ **Understand:** Explaining—Problem (Centipede was so long and thin his belly dragged on the ground.)

❷ **Understand:** Explaining (The animals were supposed to be practicing their skills.)

❸ **Understand:** Identifying—What (They were sleeping.)

❹ **Apply:** Predicting; **Create:** Generating Ideas (Centipede will find a way to get more legs . . .)

WITH THE TEACHER

Centipede went to Ant and sang a song to make Ant sleep even more deeply. Then he took one pair of Ant's legs and put them on his own body! He went to Wasp and did the same thing.

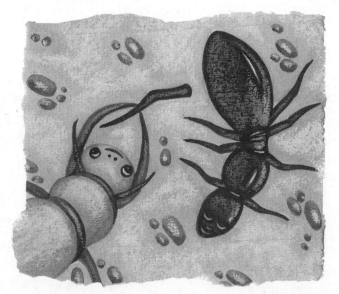

Centipede went to Beetle and Grasshopper and all the others. He took one pair of legs from each one until he had many, many legs.

Then he went to the corner of the cave where Grandmother Spider stayed. Things were different there!

Close your eyes. Listen to me read what Centipede did: He took one pair of Ant's legs and put them on his own body. What is Centipede trying to do?[1]

52

COMPREHENDING AS YOU GO

❶ Understand: Explaining—Action (Centipede is gathering legs from different insects. He will put them on his own body so his belly doesn't drag on the ground.)

5. Think and Talk

- Ask and discuss each question with your group.
- For items 4 and 5, you may wish to have students work in partners. Say something like:

For the next question, we're going to work in partners.

Remember to:
1. Listen to your partner.
2. Whisper to each other.

Listen to the next question, "How did he try to solve his problem?" Partner A, tell your partner how Centipede tried to solve his problem.

Wait, then say something like:

Partner B, add to your partner's answer. What did Centipede do?

Wait, then discuss answers with the group.

Let's all talk about our answers. [Rain], how did you and your partner answer the question?

(Centipede stole a leg from all the other insects while they were sleeping . . .)

Repeat for Question 5.

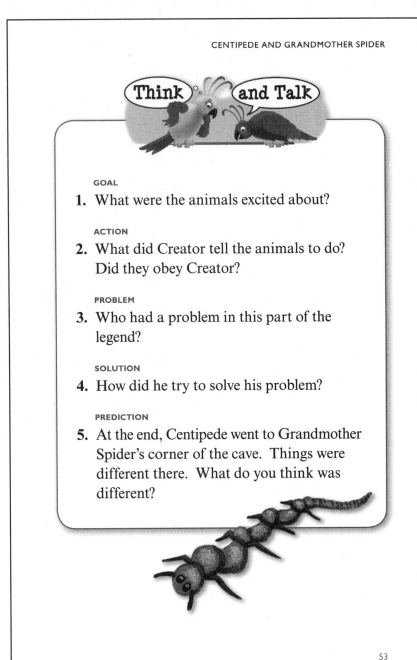

CENTIPEDE AND GRANDMOTHER SPIDER

Think and Talk

GOAL

1. What were the animals excited about?

ACTION

2. What did Creator tell the animals to do? Did they obey Creator?

PROBLEM

3. Who had a problem in this part of the legend?

SOLUTION

4. How did he try to solve his problem?

PREDICTION

5. At the end, Centipede went to Grandmother Spider's corner of the cave. Things were different there. What do you think was different?

53

❶ **Understand:** Explaining—Goal (The animals were excited because they each wanted their own place in the world.)

❷ **Understand:** Explaining—Action; Using Vocabulary—obey (Creator told the animals to practice their skills. No, they did not obey him. They slept instead.)

❸ **Understand:** Explaining—Problem (Centipede had a problem. His body was too long, and his belly dragged on the ground.)

❹ **Understand:** Explaining—Solution (Centipede stole legs from the other insects.)

❺ **Apply:** Inferring, Explaining (Grandmother Spider is probably not sleeping like the others.)

CHAPTER 3 INSTRUCTIONS

Students read Chapter 3 without the teacher, independently or with partners.

COMPREHENSION PROCESSES

Remember, Understand, Apply

PROCEDURES FOR READING ON YOUR OWN

1. Getting Ready

Have students turn to page 54.

2. Setting a Purpose

Identifying—Title; Explaining; Predicting

Before students begin reading, say something like:

Read the title of this chapter. (Grandmother Spider)

Read to find out the answers to these questions:

- What's different in Grandmother Spider's area of the cave?
- What has Grandmother Spider been doing?
- What will happen when the insects wake up?

3. Reading on Your Own: Partner or Whisper Reading

- Have students take turns reading every other page with a partner or have students whisper read on their own.
- Continue having students track each word with their fingers.
- Have students ask themselves or their partners the gray text questions.

4. Written Assessment (Comprehension and Skill Work)

Tell students they will do a Written Assessment after they read on their own. (For teacher directions, see pages 124–126.)

5. Homework 7: Repeated Reading

> **PREP NOTE**
>
> **Setting a Purpose**
>
> Write questions on a chalkboard, white board, or large piece of paper before working with your small group.

Chapter 3

Grandmother Spider

Grandmother Spider had been doing what Creator told her to do. She had not slept. She had been practicing her special skill of spinning webs. She made many webs. She knew that she and her children would be able to make a home in almost any kind of place.

54

CENTIPEDE AND GRANDMOTHER SPIDER

She practiced living in trees. She made her web between the branches and leaves. She practiced living in a hole in the ground. She made her web over the top of the hole. She made all her webs strong and very sticky.

Did Grandmother Spider *obey* Creator?**1** Where did she practice living?**2**
How do you think Grandmother Spider will be rewarded for her hard work?**3**

55

COMPREHENDING AS YOU GO

❶ **Remember:** Identifying; Using Vocabulary—obey (Grandmother Spider did obey Creator.)

❷ **Remember:** Identifying—Where (She practiced living in the trees and in a hole in the ground.)

❸ **Apply:** Predicting (She will get to pick where she wants to live. She will be able to live anywhere . . .)

ON YOUR OWN

When Centipede, with all those legs, crawled up, he got stuck in a web! He could not get away. The more he moved, the more he stuck to the threads.

56

CENTIPEDE AND GRANDMOTHER SPIDER

Grandmother Spider liked to sit at the top of her web, so she could feel anything that touched it. She felt something wiggling in her big web.

Grandmother Spider saw that Centipede was stuck in her web. She saw that he had many legs, and she knew what he had done. Grandmother Spider called out, "Wake up! Everybody, wake up! Centipede has stolen your legs!"

The insects woke up and came crawling, and buzzing, and hopping, and flying to the corner of the cave. They were angry!

Just then, Creator came. Creator said, "It is morning. It is time to go out into the world."

The insects shouted, "Look, Centipede has stolen our legs! Make him give them back!"

Creator said, "It is too late. It is morning, and you must go as you are."

What did Grandmother Spider notice about Centipede?[1] What did she do?[2]
How do the insects feel?[3]

57

COMPREHENDING AS YOU GO

[1] **Remember:** Identifying—What (Grandmother Spider noticed that Centipede had many legs.)

[2] **Remember:** Identifying—Event (She told all the other insects to wake up.)

[3] **Remember:** Identifying—How (The insects are angry!)

ON YOUR OWN

Creator said to Centipede, "Because you have done this thing, you must always hide yourself under leaves or logs or rocks."

Then Creator said to the insects, "And you insects—you slept instead of practicing your skills. You will now be food for many other animals."

Creator said to all the animals, "Now all of you—go out into the world."

So they did. To this day, Centipede hides under rocks and leaves. To this day, insects have six legs and they are eaten by other animals. To this day, Grandmother Spider sits up all night, weaving her web. She is afraid that Centipede might come and steal a pair of her eight legs.

Why does Centipede spend his days hiding under rocks?[1] Why do many animals eat the poor insects?[2] Why do spiders sit up all night weaving webs?[3]

58

COMPREHENDING AS YOU GO

❶ **Understand:** Explaining (Creator said Centipede must always hide because he took legs from the other insects.)

❷ **Understand:** Explaining (The insects slept instead of practicing, so Creator said they would be food for many other animals.)

❸ **Understand:** Explaining (Spiders sit up all night because they are afraid Centipede will come and steal their legs.)

CENTIPEDE AND GRANDMOTHER SPIDER

"That is a good story," said Gray Cloud. "Do many animals eat insects?"

Grandfather chuckled. "Insects are food for a world full of other animals."

"How do the insects survive? Won't they all get eaten up?"

"No," said the old man. "Animals are wise. They take only as much as they need, and they leave enough insects to make more."

According to Grandfather, animals are wise. What makes animals wise?[1]

59

COMPREHENDING
AS YOU GO

1 **Understand:** Explaining (Animals take only as much as they need and leave enough insects to make more.)

WRITTEN ASSESSMENT (1 of 3)

COMPREHENSION PROCESSES

Remember, Understand, Apply

WRITING TRAITS

**Conventions—Complete Sentence, Beginning Capital, Period
Presentation**

Test Taking

Unit 13 Written Assessment
Use after Exercise 8 and Centipede and Grandmother
Spider, Chapters 2 and 3

WARM-UP

| pond | underwater | swimmers | attacks | survive |

The Water Spider

Water spiders spend most of their lives under the water. All spiders breathe air, so how does the water spider survive? This is how. First, it spins a silk house on an underwater plant. Next, the spider goes to the surface. It uses small hairs on its abdomen to trap air. The spider carries the air in small bubbles to its house and puts them inside. Now the spider has air to breathe in its house.

The water spider is a carnivore. It eats insects. When an insect is near, the spider zips out and attacks. It takes the insect back to its house and has a nice meal.

Water spiders also lay their eggs in their silk homes. They even raise their babies there. The silk house is a safe place.

The water spider lives, hunts, eats, and raises its babies in a pond. It's no surprise! These spiders are great swimmers.

continued

WRITTEN ASSESSMENT (2 of 3)

Identifying—Topic

Identifying—Facts; Note Taking

Identifying—Main Idea

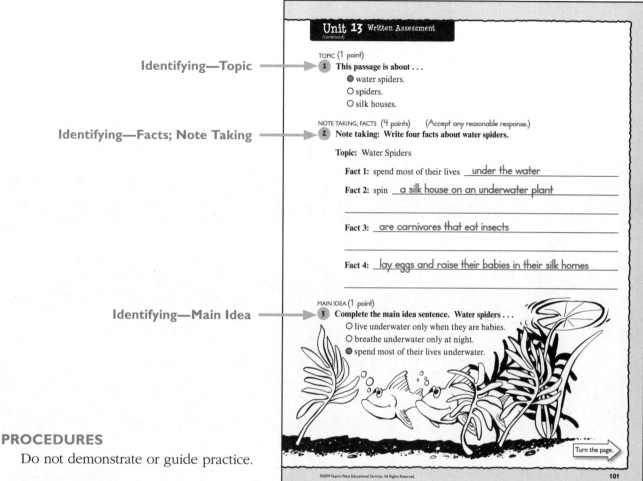

Unit 13 Written Assessment
(continued)

TOPIC (1 point)
1 **This passage is about . . .**
   ● water spiders.
   ○ spiders.
   ○ silk houses.

NOTE TAKING, FACTS (4 points)   *(Accept any reasonable response.)*
2 **Note taking: Write four facts about water spiders.**

   Topic: Water Spiders

   Fact 1: spend most of their lives ___under the water___

   Fact 2: spin ___a silk house on an underwater plant___

   Fact 3: ___are carnivores that eat insects___

   Fact 4: ___lay eggs and raise their babies in their silk homes___

MAIN IDEA (1 point)
3 **Complete the main idea sentence. Water spiders . . .**
   ○ live underwater only when they are babies.
   ○ breathe underwater only at night.
   ● spend most of their lives underwater.

Turn the page.

©2009 Sopris West Educational Services. All Rights Reserved.   101

PROCEDURES

Do not demonstrate or guide practice.

Written Assessment—Introductory Instructions

1. Introduce the Written Assessment.

   • Remind students that their work today is an opportunity for them to show what they can do independently. Say something like:
   We have been working really hard together, and you have learned many new skills and strategies. I'm very proud of you. Today, you get to show me what you can do all by yourself.

   • Tell students they will whisper read the passage and then answer the questions without help.

   You're going to whisper read a passage and then answer the questions—just like you've been doing on your Comprehension and Skill Work. The only thing different is that you need to work by yourself.
   If you read a question and aren't sure what to do, reread the question and try again.
   What should you do if you can't answer a question? (Reread the question and try again.)
   If you still can't answer the question, reread the passage and try again.
   What should you do if you still can't answer a question?
   (Reread the passage and try again.)
   If you still aren't sure, just do your best.

> **NOTE**
> Students may have taken Written Assessments in Units 5–12. If so, modify instructions, as appropriate.

WRITTEN ASSESSMENT (3 of 3)

Using Vocabulary—protected

Sequencing; Identifying—Events;
Sentence Completion

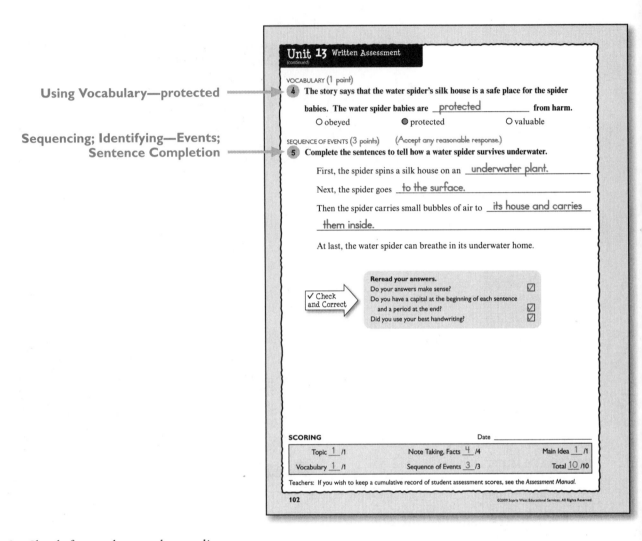

Unit 13 Written Assessment
(continued)

VOCABULARY (1 point)

4. The story says that the water spider's silk house is a safe place for the spider babies. The water spider babies are ___protected___ from harm.

    ○ obeyed   ● protected   ○ valuable

SEQUENCE OF EVENTS (3 points)   (Accept any reasonable response.)

5. Complete the sentences to tell how a water spider survives underwater.

First, the spider spins a silk house on an ___underwater plant.___

Next, the spider goes ___to the surface.___

Then the spider carries small bubbles of air to ___its house and carries them inside.___

At last, the water spider can breathe in its underwater home.

✓ Check and Correct

Reread your answers.
Do your answers make sense?   ☑
Do you have a capital at the beginning of each sentence
   and a period at the end?   ☑
Did you use your best handwriting?   ☑

SCORING   Date _____

| Topic _1_ /1 | Note Taking, Facts _4_ /4 | Main Idea _1_ /1 |
| Vocabulary _1_ /1 | Sequence of Events _3_ /3 | Total _10_ /10 |

Teachers: If you wish to keep a cumulative record of student assessment scores, see the *Assessment Manual*.

102   ©2009 Sopris West Educational Services. All Rights Reserved.

2. Check for student understanding.
   Say something like:
   Look at your assessment. What are you going to do first? (Write my name.)
   What are going to do next? (Whisper read the passage.)
   What will you do after you read the passage? (Answer the questions.)
   That's great. Now what will you do if you get to a hard question?
   (Reread the question and try again.)
   That's right. What should you do if it's still hard? (Reread the passage and try again.)
   Very good. And if you still aren't sure, what will you do? (Do my best and keep going.)

3. Remind students to check and correct.
   When you finish your assessment, what should you do? (Check and correct.)
   That's right. Go to the top of the page. Reread the questions and make sure your answers make sense. Fix anything that doesn't sound right. Make sure you have an answer for every question.

4. Remind students what to do when they finish their work.

End of the Unit

In this section, you will find:

Making Decisions

As you near the end of the unit, plan to give the Written Assessment and the Oral Reading Fluency Assessment to each child in your group. Use this section as a general guide for making instructional decisions and doing diagnostic planning.

Written Assessment

The Unit 13 Written Assessment is located on page 99 of *Activity Book 3* and on the CD.

Oral Reading Fluency Assessment

The Unit 13 Oral Reading Fluency Assessment is located on page 131 of this teacher's guide and in the *Assessment Manual*.

Certificate of Achievement

Celebrate your children's accomplishments. When your students master the unit skills, send home the Certificate of Achievement.

Extra Practice Lessons

Use the Extra Practice lessons for students who need additional decoding and fluency work. Student materials can be copied from the Extra Practice blackline masters.

Making Decisions

1. After students read Story Reading 7, "Centipede and Grandmother Spider," Chapters 2 and 3, give the group the Unit 13 Written Assessment in place of Comprehension and Skill Work. Follow the instructions on pages 124–126 of this guide.

2. While the group is completing the Written Assessment or any time during the day, administer the Oral Reading Fluency Assessment. Assess each student individually.

    Optional: Graph the results of the assessment. (See Unit 7 Teacher's Guide, pages 92 and 95.)
    • If the student's words correct per minute go up, congratulate the student.
    • If the student's words correct per minute go down, discuss the student's overall improvement and help him or her identify ways to improve for the next assessment.

3. Score oral fluency responses on the Student Assessment Record. Adhere to the scoring criteria in the *Assessment Manual*. Use a stopwatch to time how long it takes each student to read the Oral Reading Fluency Passage, and record errors.

USING WRITTEN ASSESSMENT RESULTS

Results of the Written Assessment *should not* be used to determine whether a student or group of students continues forward in the program. As long as students pass the Oral Reading Fluency Assessment, they should continue forward with the next unit.

The Written Assessment should be used to informally monitor how well students read independently and answer questions in writing. If any student has difficulty with the Written Assessment, re-administer the assessment orally.

If the student has difficulty answering the questions orally:
• Record the types of errors (e.g., main idea, sequencing, open-ended response).
• Provide explicit instruction for these types of questions during reading group, before independent work, and in tutorials, as needed.
    1) Demonstrate (or model) appropriate responses, guide practice, and provide opportunities for independent practice.
    2) For inferential questions, think aloud with students—explain how you arrive at an answer.
    3) For literal questions, teach students to reread a passage, locate information, reread the question, and respond.

USING THE ORAL READING FLUENCY RESULTS

At the end of each unit, you will need to make decisions regarding student progress. Should students go forward in the program? Does the group need Extra Practice before proceeding? Do individuals require more assistance and practice to continue working in their group? These decisions all require use of the oral reading fluency data and professional judgment. As you analyze assessment results, watch for trends and anomalies.

See the *Assessment Manual* for detailed information and instructional recommendations. General guidelines and recommendations follow:

Strong Pass ≥ 114 WCPM 0–2 errors	• Continue with the current pace of instruction. • Have students set goals. (Until students are reading approximately 180 words correct per minute, oral reading fluency continues to be an instructional goal.)
Pass 93–113 WCPM 0–2 errors	• Continue with the current pace of instruction. Consider increasing fluency practice.
No Pass ≤ 92 WCPM	• If a child scores a No Pass but has previously passed all assessments, you may wish to advance the student to the next unit, then carefully monitor the student. • If a child scores a No Pass but has previously passed all assessments, you may wish to advance the student to the next unit and also provide additional practice opportunities. (See below.) • If a child scores two consecutive No Passes or periodic No Passes, additional practice must be provided. (See below.) • If a child scores three consecutive No Passes, the student should be placed in a lower-performing group.

RED FLAG
A No Pass is a red flag. A mild early intervention can prevent an intense and time-consuming intervention in the future.

Added Practice Options for Groups

Warm-Ups:
- Begin each lesson with Partner Reading of the previous day's homework.
- Begin each day with Partner Reading of a Word Fluency from Extra Practice.
- Begin each lesson with a five-minute Fluency Booster. Place copies of the Unit 7–12 *Read Well* Homework in three-ring notebooks. Each day, have students begin Finger Tracking and Whisper Reading at Unit 7, Homework 1. At the end of five minutes, have students mark where they are in their notebooks. The next day, the goal is to read farther.
- Begin each Story Reading with a review of the previous day's story.
- After reading the story, include Short Passage Practice on a daily basis.

Extended Units: If several children begin to score No Passes or barely pass, extend the unit by adding Extra Practices 1, 2, and/or 3. Extra Practice lessons include Decoding Practice, Fluency Passage, Word Fluency, and a Comprehension and Skill Activity. (See pages 134–140 in this guide.)

Jell-Well Reviews: A Jell-Well Review is the *Read Well* term for a review of earlier units. A Jell-Well Review is a period of time taken to celebrate what children have learned and an opportunity to firm up their foundation of learning. To complete a Jell-Well Review, take the group back to the last unit for which all students scored Strong Passes. Then quickly cycle back up. See the *Assessment Manual* for how to build a Jell-Well Review.

Added Practice Options for Individual Students

Tutorials: Set up five-minute tutorials on a daily basis with an assistant, trained volunteer, or cross-age tutor. Have the tutor provide Short Passage Practice and Timed Readings or Extra Practice lessons.

Double Dose: Find ways to provide a double dose of *Read Well* instruction.
- Have the student work in his or her group *and* a lower-performing group.
- Have an instructional assistant, older student, or parent volunteer preview or review lessons.
- Have an instructional assistant provide instruction with Extra Practice lessons.
- Preview new lessons or review previous lessons.

END-OF-THE-UNIT CELEBRATION

When students pass the Oral Reading Fluency Assessment, celebrate with the Certificate of Achievement on page 132.

Note: Using the Flesch-Kincaid Grade Level readability formula, the Unit 13 Assessment has a 2.7 readability level. Readabilities are based on number of words per sentence and number of syllables per word. Adding one or two multisyllabic words can increase readability by a month or two. Though we are attending to readability for the assessments, the overriding factor is decodability.

TRICKY WORD and FOCUS SKILL WARM-UP

screeched	watched	sparkled	Grandfather	climbed

ORAL READING FLUENCY PASSAGE

Gray Cloud and Grandfather

★It was going to be an amazing day. Gray Cloud could   11
see the sun peeking over the mountains. Shadow and light filled   22
the clearing where Grandfather's wigwam stood. Birds began to   31
sing in the great pine trees at the edge of the meadow. Dewdrops   44
sparkled on the tall green grass.   50

Gray Cloud put one knee down on the ground and   60
watched a spider spin its web. As the sun slowly climbed higher   72
in the sky, the buzzing sound of insects grew louder and louder.   84
A raven screeched. Gray Cloud looked up.   91

Grandfather stood beside him. "You are a good boy, Gray   101
Cloud. You see with both eyes at once, and you listen with both   114
ears at once."   117

Gray Cloud smiled and jumped to his feet. It was a   128
perfect day for a long hike. He and Grandfather started walking   139
down the sunny trail.   143

ORAL READING FLUENCY	Start timing at the ★. Mark errors. Make a single slash in the text (/) at 60 seconds. Have the student complete the passage. If the student completes the passage in less than 60 seconds, have the student go back to the ★ and continue reading. Make a double slash (//) in the text at 60 seconds.
WCPM	Determine words correct per minute by subtracting errors from words read in 60 seconds.
STRONG PASS	The student scores no more than 2 errors on the first pass through the passage and reads 114 or more words correct per minute. Proceed to Unit 14.
PASS	The student scores no more than 2 errors on the first pass through the passage and reads 93 to 113 words correct per minute. Proceed to Unit 14.
NO PASS	The student scores 3 or more errors on the first pass through the passage and/or reads 92 or fewer words correct per minute. Provide added fluency practice with *RW2* Unit 13 Extra Practice. (Lessons follow the certificate at the end of the teacher's guide.) After completing the Extra Practice, retest the student.

Spider Scholar!

_____

successfully completed

Read Well 2 Unit 13 • *Spiders*

with _____ words correct per minute and
wrote a fascinating report about spiders.

Teacher Signature _____

Date _____

✂ -

Spider Scholar!

_____

successfully completed

Read Well 2 Unit 13 • *Spiders*

with _____ words correct per minute and
wrote a fascinating report about spiders.

Teacher Signature _____

Date _____

PROCEDURES

1. Sound Review
Use selected Sound Cards from Units 1–13.

2. Sounding Out Smoothly
- For each word, have students say the underlined part, sound out the word smoothly, then read the whole word. (Use the words in sentences, as needed.)
- Have students read all the words in the row, building accuracy first, then fluency.
- Repeat practice.

3. Accuracy and Fluency Building
- For each task, have students say any underlined part, then read each word.
- Set a pace. Then have students read the whole words in each task and column.
- Repeat practice, building accuracy first, then fluency.

4. Tricky Words
Have students read each row for accuracy, then fluency.

5. Multisyllabic Words
For each word, have students read each syllable out loud, then tell how many syllables are in the word. If needed, use the word in a sentence. Have students read the whole word.

6. Dictation

orb, for, forth, furry, hurry, scurry
- Say "orb." Have students say the word. Have students touch or write the sounds, then read the word. Say something like:

  The first word is **orb.** Say the word. (orb)

  What's the first sound? (/or/) Write /or/ using the o-r pattern.

  What's the last sound? (/b/) Touch under /b/.

- Repeat with "for" and "forth."
- Continue with the rhyming words: furry, hurry, scurry.

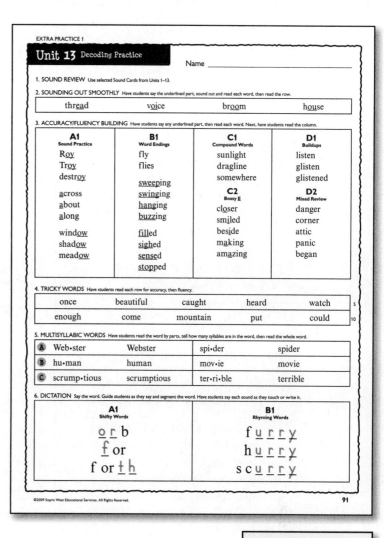

CAUTION

Your children may not need Extra Practice. Use assessment results to determine if Extra Practice is needed.

PROCEDURES

1. First Reading

Mix group and individual turns, independent of your voice.

2. Second Reading, Short Passage Practice: Developing Prosody

• Demonstrate how to read a line or two with expression. Read at a rate slightly faster than the students' rate. Say something like:

Listen as I read the first two sentences with expression and phrasing. I'm going to emphasize certain words and pause between sentences.

"Webster had spun a beautiful web across the attic window. The silk threads glistened in the sunlight."

• Guide practice with your voice.
Now read the paragraph with me.

• Provide individual turns while others track with their fingers and whisper read.
Provide descriptive and positive feedback.
[Alexis], you read with wonderful expression!

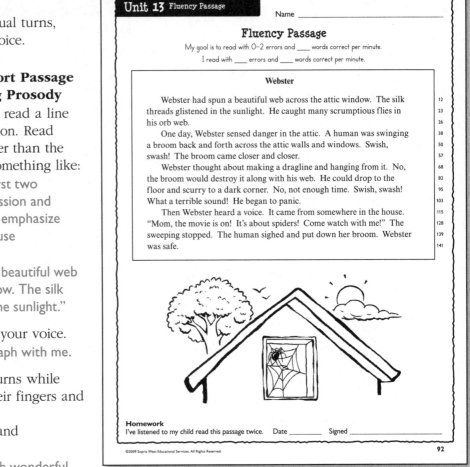

Unit 13 Fluency Passage

Name _____

Fluency Passage

My goal is to read with 0–2 errors and ____ words correct per minute.

I read with ____ errors and ____ words correct per minute.

Webster

   Webster had spun a beautiful web across the attic window. The silk threads glistened in the sunlight. He caught many scrumptious flies in his orb web. — 12, 23, 26

   One day, Webster sensed danger in the attic. A human was swinging a broom back and forth across the attic walls and windows. Swish, swash! The broom came closer and closer. — 38, 50, 57

   Webster thought about making a dragline and hanging from it. No, the broom would destroy it along with his web. He could drop to the floor and scurry to a dark corner. No, not enough time. Swish, swash! What a terrible sound! He began to panic. — 68, 82, 95, 103

   Then Webster heard a voice. It came from somewhere in the house. "Mom, the movie is on! It's about spiders! Come watch with me!" The sweeping stopped. The human sighed and put down her broom. Webster was safe. — 115, 128, 139, 141

Homework
I've listened to my child read this passage twice.   Date _____   Signed _____

92

3. Partner Reading: Repeated Reading (Checkout Opportunity)

 While students do Partner Reading, listen to individuals read the passage. Work on accuracy and fluency, as needed.

4. Homework: Repeated Reading

 Have students read the story at home.

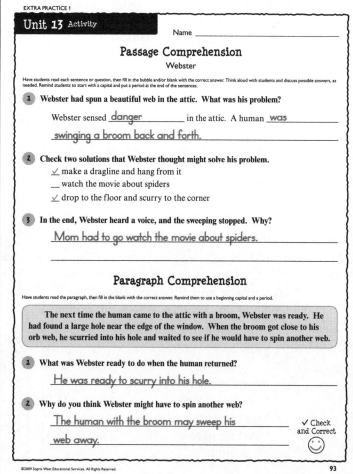

EXTRA PRACTICE

Unit 13 Word Fluency A

Name _____

Rhyming Words

High-Frequency Rhyming Words: boy, enjoy, stay, day, may, play, away, ride, side, wide, divide

boy	joy	toy	soy	enjoy
oar	soar	roar	boar	uproar
stay	day	may	play	away
ride	slide	side	wide	divide
foil	broil	toil	spoil	turmoil

Related Words

color	colors	colored	coloring	colorful
divide	divided	dividing	division	divisible
sharp	sharper	sharpest	sharpen	sharpener
depend	depended	depending	dependent	independent
move	moved	mover	movement	remove

High-Frequency Tricky Words

listen	covered	several	toward	against
against	several	toward	listen	covered
toward	listen	covered	against	several
covered	toward	against	several	listen
several	against	listen	covered	toward

©2009 Sopris West Educational Services. All Rights Reserved.

Available on CD-ROM

EXTRA PRACTICE 1

Unit 13 Activity

Name _____

Passage Comprehension
Webster

Have students read each sentence or question, then fill in the bubble and/or blank with the correct answer. Think aloud with students and discuss possible answers, as needed. Remind students to start with a capital and put a period at the end of the sentences.

1 Webster had spun a beautiful web in the attic. What was his problem?

Webster sensed _danger_ in the attic. A human _was_ _swinging a broom back and forth._

2 Check two solutions that Webster thought might solve his problem.
   ✓ make a dragline and hang from it
   _ watch the movie about spiders
   ✓ drop to the floor and scurry to the corner

3 In the end, Webster heard a voice, and the sweeping stopped. Why?

Mom had to go watch the movie about spiders.

Paragraph Comprehension

Have students read the paragraph, then fill in the blank with the correct answer. Remind them to use a beginning capital and a period.

> The next time the human came to the attic with a broom, Webster was ready. He had found a large hole near the edge of the window. When the broom got close to his orb web, he scurried into his hole and waited to see if he would have to spin another web.

1 What was Webster ready to do when the human returned?

He was ready to scurry into his hole.

2 Why do you think Webster might have to spin another web?

The human with the broom may sweep his _web away._

✓ Check and Correct ☺

©2009 Sopris West Educational Services. All Rights Reserved.   93

PROCEDURES

For each step, demonstrate and guide practice, as needed. Then have students complete the page independently.

1. Activity
Passage Comprehension
- Have students read each sentence or question, then fill in or check the blank with the correct answer.
- Think aloud with students and discuss the multiple-choice options, as needed.

Paragraph Comprehension
- Have students read the paragraph.
- Have students read each numbered question, then answer the question with a complete sentence.
- Have students read the completed sentences.

Self-monitoring
Have students read and check their work, then draw a happy face in the Check and Correct circle.

2. Word Fluency (BLMs are located on the CD.)
- To build fluency, have students read Rhyming Words, Related Words, and High-Frequency Tricky Words. Have students read each section three times in a row.
- To build accuracy, have students read all sets with partners.

PROCEDURES

1. Sound Review

Use selected Sound Cards from Units 1–13.

2. Sounding Out Smoothly

- For each word, have students say the underlined part, sound out the word smoothly, then read the whole word. (Use the words in sentences, as needed.)
- Have students read all the words in the row, building accuracy first, then fluency.
- Repeat practice.

3. Accuracy and Fluency Building

- For each task, have students say any underlined part, then read each word.
- Set a pace. Then have students read the whole words in each task and column.
- Provide repeated practice, building accuracy first, then fluency.

4. Tricky Words

Have students read each row for accuracy, then fluency.

5. Multisyllabic Words

For each word, have students read each syllable out loud, then tell how many syllables are in the word. If needed, use the word in a sentence. Have students read the whole word.

6. Dictation

sky, try, type, dewdrop, raindrop, teardrop

- Say "sky." Have students say the word. Have students touch or write the sounds, then read the word. The first word is **sky.** Say the word. (sky)

  What's the first sound? (/sss/) Touch under /sss/.
  What's the next sound? (/k/) Touch under /k/.
  What's the next sound? (/īīī/) Write /īīī/ with the letter . . . y.
  Read the word. (sky)

- Repeat with "try" and "type."
- Continue with the rhyming words: dewdrop, raindrop, teardrop.

EXTRA PRACTICE 2

Unit 13 Decoding Practice

Name _____

1. SOUND REVIEW Use selected Sound Cards from Units 1–13.

2. SOUNDING OUT SMOOTHLY Have students say the underlined part, sound out and read each word, then read the row.

f<u>a</u>ngs	grow	pair	sp<u>e</u>nd

3. ACCURACY/FLUENCY BUILDING Have students say any underlined part, then read each word. Next, have students read the column.

A1 Sound Practice	**B1** Word Endings	**C1** Word Endings	**D1** Compound Words
b<u>oy</u>	body	<u>higher</u>	Grandfather
j<u>oy</u>	bodies	<u>louder</u>	themselves
enj<u>oy</u>		bigger	**D2** Mixed Practice
<u>o</u>ver	wiggle	lar<u>gest</u>	
pr<u>o</u>tect	wiggling	<u>quickly</u>	<u>inches</u>
b<u>o</u>th	drop	<u>slowly</u>	<u>insects</u>
	dropping	**C2** Rhyming Words	<u>spiders</u>
places			<u>segments</u>
r<u>a</u>ven	<u>darkness</u>	<u>rock</u>	<u>wigwams</u>
prey	<u>peeking</u>	<u>block</u>	<u>hundreds</u>
	<u>attacks</u>	<u>knock</u>	<u>thousands</u>

4. TRICKY WORDS Have students read each row for accuracy, then fluency.

listen	climbed	come	other	don't	5
have	eyes	great	there	where	10

5. MULTISYLLABIC WORDS Have students read the word by parts, tell how many syllables are in the word, then read the whole word.

Ⓐ	poi•son	poison	per•fect	perfect
Ⓑ	un•der•neath	underneath	pred•a•tor	predator
Ⓒ	car•ni•vores	carnivores	cen•ti•pede	centipede

6. DICTATION Say the word. Guide students as they say and segment the word. Have students say each sound as they touch or write it.

A1 Shifty Words	**B1** Rhyming Words
s k <u>y</u>	d e w d r <u>o</u> p
t <u>r</u> y	r a i n d r <u>o</u> p
t y <u>p</u> e	t e a r d r <u>o</u> p

94

> **CAUTION**
>
> Your children may not need Extra Practice. Use assessment results to determine if Extra Practice is needed.

PROCEDURES • FLUENCY

1. First Reading

Mix group and individual turns, independent of your voice. Have students work toward an accuracy goal of 0–2 errors and practice any difficult words.

2. Second Reading, Timed Reading: Repeated Reading

- Once the group accuracy goal has been achieved, time individual students for 30 or 60 seconds while the other children track with their fingers and whisper read.

- Determine words correct per minute. Record student scores. Celebrate when students reach their goals!

  Wow! [Logan], you met your goal. That was your best score ever. You get to read to the principal this week.

3. Partner Reading: Repeated Reading (Checkout Opportunity)

While students do Partner Reading, listen to individuals read the passage. Work on accuracy and fluency, as needed.

4. Homework: Repeated Reading

Have students read the story at home.

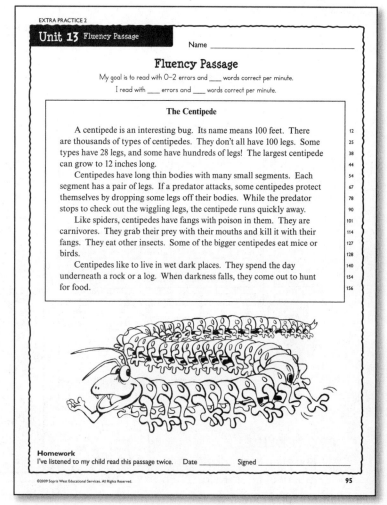

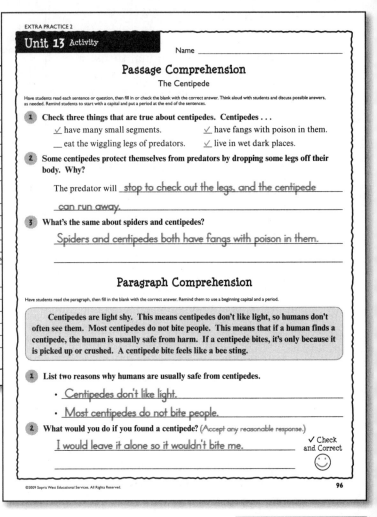

EXTRA PRACTICE

Unit 13 Word Fluency B

Name _____

Rhyming Words

High-Frequency Rhyming Words: an, than, can, man, began, song, long, strong, wrong, along, old, told, cold, hold, sen, let, yet, all, call, small, fall

an	than	can	man	began
song	long	strong	wrong	along
old	told	cold	hold	withhold
met	set	let	yet	fishnet
all	call	small	fall	baseball

Related Words

locate	located	locating	location	relocate
protect	protected	unprotected	protecting	protection
value	valuable	invaluable	evaluation	evaluating
taste	tasted	tasting	tasty	tasteless
poison	poisoned	poisoning	poisonous	nonpoisonous

High-Frequency Tricky Words

numeral	table	money	pulled	cried
money	numeral	table	cried	pulled
cried	money	pulled	table	numeral
table	pulled	cried	numeral	money
pulled	cried	numeral	money	table

©2009 Sopris West Educational Services. All Rights Reserved.

Available on CD-ROM

EXTRA PRACTICE 2

Unit 13 Activity

Name _____

Passage Comprehension
The Centipede

Have students read each sentence or question, then fill in or check the blank with the correct answer. Think aloud with students and discuss possible answers, as needed. Remind students to start with a capital and put a period at the end of the sentences.

1 Check three things that are true about centipedes. Centipedes . . .

✓ have many small segments.   ✓ have fangs with poison in them.

__ eat the wiggling legs of predators.   ✓ live in wet dark places.

2 Some centipedes protect themselves from predators by dropping some legs off their body. Why?

The predator will _stop to check out the legs, and the centipede can run away._

3 What's the same about spiders and centipedes?

Spiders and centipedes both have fangs with poison in them.

Paragraph Comprehension

Have students read the paragraph, then fill in the blank with the correct answer. Remind them to use a beginning capital and a period.

> Centipedes are light shy. This means centipedes don't like light, so humans don't often see them. Most centipedes do not bite people. This means that if a human finds a centipede, the human is usually safe from harm. If a centipede bites, it's only because it is picked up or crushed. A centipede bite feels like a bee sting.

1 List two reasons why humans are usually safe from centipedes.

• _Centipedes don't like light._

• _Most centipedes do not bite people._

2 What would you do if you found a centipede? (Accept any reasonable response.)

I would leave it alone so it wouldn't bite me.

✓ Check and Correct ☺

©2009 Sopris West Educational Services. All Rights Reserved.   96

PROCEDURES

For each step, demonstrate and guide practice, as needed. Then have students complete the page independently.

1. Activity
Passage Comprehension

- Have students read each sentence or question, then fill in or check the blank with the correct answer.
- Think aloud with students and discuss the multiple-choice options, as needed.

Paragraph Comprehension

- Have students read the paragraph.
- Have students read each numbered sentence, then fill in the blank with a complete sentence.
- Have students read the completed sentences.

Self-monitoring

Have students read and check their work, then draw a happy face in the Check and Correct circle.

2. Word Fluency (BLMs are located on the CD.)

- To build fluency, have students read Rhyming Words, Related Words, and High-Frequency Tricky Words. Have students read each section three times in a row.
- To build accuracy, have students read all sets with partners.

> **ACCURACY BEFORE FLUENCY**
> **(Reminder)**
> Word Fluency is designed to build accuracy and fluency. Students should practice for accuracy before working on fluency.

PROCEDURES

1. Sound Review

Use selected Sound Cards from Units 1–13.

2. Sounding Out Smoothly

- For each word, have students say the underlined part, sound out the word smoothly, then read the whole word.
- Have students read all the words in the row.
- Repeat practice. Mix group and individual turns, independent of your voice.

3. Accuracy and Fluency Building

- For each task, have students say any underlined part, then read each word.
- Set a pace. Then have students read the whole words in each task and column.

4. Tricky Words

Have students read each row for accuracy, then fluency.

5. Multisyllabic Words

For each word, have students read each syllable out loud, then tell how many syllables are in the word. If needed, use the word in a sentence. Have students read the whole word.

6. Dictation

bites, bikes, hikes, good, stood, wood

- Say "bites." Have students say the word. Have students touch or write the sounds, then read the word. Say something like:

  The first word is **bites.** Say the word. (bites)

  What's the first sound? (/b/) Touch under /b/.
  What's the next sound? (/īīī/) Write /īīī/.
  What's the next sound? (/t/) Touch under /t/.
  What's the last sound? (/sss/) Touch under /s/. Read the word. (bites)
  Yes, the Bossy E at the end makes the letter i say its name.

- Repeat with "bikes" and "hikes."
- Continue with the rhyming words: good, stood, wood.

EXTRA PRACTICE 3

Unit 13 Decoding Practice

Name _____

1. SOUND REVIEW Use selected Sound Cards from Units 1–13.

2. SOUNDING OUT SMOOTHLY Have students say the underlined part, sound out and read each word, then read the row.

| edge | grew | cl<u>ea</u>r | tr<u>ai</u>l |

3. ACCURACY/FLUENCY BUILDING Have students say any underlined part, then read each word. Next, have students read the column.

A1 Sound Practice	B1 Word Endings	C1 Rhyming Words	D1 Related Words
b<u>oy</u>	<u>hair</u>s	ni<u>ce</u>	fascinate
enj<u>oy</u>	hairy	sli<u>ce</u>	fascinated
destr<u>oy</u>		advi<u>ce</u>	fascinating
A2 Mixed Practice	itch	**C2** Bossy E	**D2** Compound Words
<u>a</u>lso	itches	pla<u>ce</u>s	underground
body	itchy	th<u>e</u>se	grasshoppers
des<u>er</u>t	sun	p<u>i</u>ne	Grandfather
cri<u>ck</u>ets	sunny	h<u>o</u>le	dewdrops
	sparkled	h<u>u</u>ge	
	screeched		

4. TRICKY WORDS Have students read each row for accuracy, then fluency.

| his | has | gives | special | warm | 5 |
| water | was | mountain | once | don't | 10 |

5. MULTISYLLABIC WORDS Have students read the word by parts, tell how many syllables are in the word, then read the whole word.

Ⓐ	mead·ow	meadow	crea·ture	creature
Ⓑ	wan·ders	wanders	vi·bra·tions	vibrations
Ⓒ	ab·do·men	abdomen	ta·ran·tu·las	tarantulas

6. DICTATION Say the word. Guide students as they say and segment the word. Have students say each sound as they touch or write it.

A1 Shifty Words	B1 Rhyming Words
b <u>i</u> t e s	g <u>o o</u> d
b <u>i</u> k e s	s t <u>o o</u> d
<u>h</u> i k e s	w <u>o o</u> d

©2009 Sopris West Educational Services. All Rights Reserved.   97

CAUTION

Your children may not need Extra Practice. Use assessment results to determine if Extra Practice is needed.

PROCEDURES • FLUENCY PASSAGE

1. First Reading
Have students work toward an accuracy goal of 0–2 errors.

2. Second Reading, Short Passage Practice: Developing Prosody
- Demonstrate and guide how to read a line or two.
- Provide individual turns while others track with their fingers and whisper read.

3. Partner Reading: Repeated Reading (Checkout Opportunity)

 While students do Partner Reading, listen to individuals read the passage. Work on accuracy and fluency, as needed.

4. Homework: Repeated Reading

 Have students read the story at home.

PROCEDURES • ACTIVITY, WORD FLUENCY A OR B

1. Activity
Passage Comprehension
Have students read each sentence or question, then fill in the blank with the correct answer.

Paragraph Comprehension
- Have students read the paragraph.
- Have students read each item, then fill in the blanks.
- Have students read the completed sentence.

2. Word Fluency (BLMs are located on the CD.)
You may wish to have students repeat practice with Extra Practice, Word Fluency A or B.

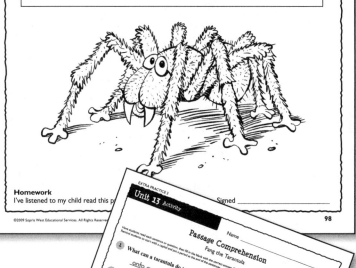

EXTRA PRACTICE 3

Unit 13 Fluency Passage

Name _____

Fluency Passage

My goal is to read with 0–2 errors and ____ words correct per minute.

I read with ____ errors and ____ words correct per minute.

Fang the Tarantula

Jack has a pet tarantula. Her name is Fang. She is huge and hairy. | 14
Her body is about three inches long. The hairs on her body let her sense | 29
vibrations. She also has special hairs on her legs that she can rub onto a | 44
predator. These hairs make the predator very itchy! | 52

Tarantulas live in the desert and other hot places. They don't like the | 65
cold. Jack keeps Fang's cage in a nice warm place so she feels at home. | 80
Jack also keeps dirt in Fang's cage so she can dig a hole in the dirt. | 96
Tarantulas like to live underground. | 101

Jack gives his spider water to drink. He puts grasshoppers, crickets, | 112
and other insects in her cage. When one of these insects wanders past her | 126
hole, Fang jumps out and grabs it. Then she bites it with her fangs. Fang | 141
is a fascinating creature! | 145

Homework
I've listened to my child read this p...   Signed _____

98

EXTRA PRACTICE 3

Unit 13 Activity

Name _____

Passage Comprehension
Fang the Tarantula

Have students read each sentence or question, then fill in the blank with the correct answer. Think aloud with students and discuss possible answers, as needed. Remind students to start with a capital and put a period at the end of the sentence.

1. What can a tarantula do to stop a predator? A tarantula can _rub special hairs_ _onto a predator to make it itchy._

2. Pets like to feel at home. What does Jack do to keep Fang happy?
Jack keeps Fang's cage _in a nice warm place._

3. What does Jack also do?
Jack also _keeps dirt in Fang's cage._

4. What does Fang do when Jack puts grasshoppers and crickets in the cage?
Fang jumps out of her hole and bites the insect with _her fangs._

Paragraph Comprehension

Have students read the paragraph, then fill in the blank with the correct answer. Remind them to start with a beginning capital and a period.

Tarantulas are both predators and prey. Lizards, snakes, and spider-eating birds eat tarantulas. The large blue, green, and red wasp called the tarantula hawk is a tarantula's most feared enemy. It stings the tarantula and then lays its eggs inside the tarantula's body!

1. List three animals that eat tarantulas.
- _lizards_
- _snakes_
- _birds_

2. Why does a tarantula fear the blue, green, and red wasp?
The wasp _stings the tarantula, then lays its eggs_ _inside the tarantula._

✓ Check and Correct

99